Supporting Spelling

More titles in the *Helping Hands* series:

Supporting Reading by Angela Wilson and Julie Scanlon, ISBN 1-84312-210-3

Supporting Speaking and Listening by Angela Wilson, ISBN 1-84312-211-1

Supporting Writing by Sylvia Edwards, ISBN 1-84312-209-X

A selection of other books for teaching assistants:

A Handbook for Learning Support Assistants: Teachers and Assistants Working Together by Glenys Fox, ISBN 1-84312-081-X

Assisting Learning and Supporting Teaching: A Practical Guide for the Teaching Assistant in the Classroom by Anne Watkinson, ISBN 1-85346-794-4

Supporting Children with Behaviour Difficulties: A Guide for Assistants in Schools by Glenys Fox, ISBN 1-85346-764-2

The Essential Guide for Competent Teaching Assistants: Meeting the National Occupational Standards at Level 2 by Anne Watkinson, ISBN 1-84312-008-9

The Essential Guide for Experienced Teaching Assistants: Meeting the National Occupational Standards at Level 3 by Anne Watkinson, ISBN 1-84312-009-7

Successful Study: Skills for Teaching Assistants by Christine Ritchie and Paul Thomas, ISBN 1-84312-106-9

Understanding Children's Learning: A Text for Teaching Assistants edited by Claire Alfrey, ISBN 1-84312-069-0

Supporting Spelling

Sylvia Edwards

Series edited by Sylvia Edwards and Angela Wilson

 David Fulton Publishers

David Fulton Publishers Ltd
The Chiswick Centre, 414 Chiswick High Road, London W4 5TF

www.fultonpublishers.co.uk

First published in Great Britain in 2004 by David Fulton Publishers.

10 9 8 7 6 5 4 3 2 1

Note: The right of Sylvia Edwards to be identified as the author of this work has been asserted by her in accordance with the Copyright, Designs and Patents Act 1988.

Copyright © Sylvia Edwards 2004

British Library Cataloguing in Publication Data
A catalogue record for this book is available from the British Library.

David Fulton Publishers is a division of Granada Learning, part of ITV plc.

ISBN 1 84312 208 1

Typeset by FiSH Books
Printed and bound in Great Britain

Contents

Introduction

Supporting Spelling provides a wealth of information and advice on how to develop spelling skills and is intended as a basic handbook for all staff involved in teaching or supporting children's spelling.

The government's strategy for primary schools aims to ensure that 'excellence and enjoyment' underpin teaching and learning. Key to the strategy's success is the need for increasing numbers of support staff, used in a way that helps to improve standards (DfES 2003). The government's strategy also refers to higher-level teaching assistants (HLTAs) who will undertake a more responsible role in raising pupil achievement. I hope that this book will help all teaching assistant staff, those who are relatively inexperienced as well as those at HLTA level, to support and enhance spelling development effectively.

Spelling is a key area of literacy and one in which teaching assistants are expected to work independently with individuals and groups of children at all levels of ability and attainment. While this book is aimed at teaching assistants, it will also be of value to other staff involved in developing spelling. Parents too may find the information useful and stimulating in helping them to support their child's spelling at home.

The book reflects an inclusive approach to teaching spelling in line with the National Curriculum (DfEE 1995) and is organised around the National Literacy Strategy (NLS) objectives for spelling (NLS 2001), now part of the Primary Strategy. For the purpose of this book the term 'NLS' will be used to refer to the above.

Spelling is a complex area of learning and it is little wonder that many children struggle, even as they reach the threshold of adulthood, to become competent spellers. This book is intended to support all children's spelling within an inclusive context, but cannot specifically address issues linked with special educational needs (SEN). However, brief references to SEN and/or related legislation may be included where relevant.

The book focuses on Key Stages 1 and 2, but the principles for learning how to spell can be applied equally to children in Key Stage 3, many of whom still require additional support for spelling. The advice will therefore be of use to secondary staff. The development of handwriting is also included as difficulties with letter formation can form a major barrier to spelling progress.

Finally, *Supporting Spelling* encourages readers to understand the principles on which spelling is based in order to make more informed choices for the benefit of the learners they support.

Chapter 1

Responding to national requirements

This chapter has three aims:

- To raise awareness of the National Curriculum statements for inclusion as the basis of an inclusive spelling approach.
- To summarise briefly the requirements of the National Curriculum for spelling at Key Stages 1 and 2.
- To introduce the NLS objectives for spelling which underpin the practical strategies and resources contained in the book.

Given that the National Curriculum level descriptions state the criteria by which children's spelling competence is assessed, it helps if all professionals are aware of what these are. Knowing *what* is to be assessed will enable us to consider *how* to develop the relevant skills and competences.

The National Curriculum inclusion statement

The following three principles suggest how all children can be effectively included within the curriculum; they underpin all aspects of teaching and learning. Let's think about each one in relation to spelling.

1. *Setting suitable challenges* so that 'all learners should experience success and achieve as high a standard as possible' (DfEE 1995). The National Curriculum supports a flexible approach so that all children can be challenged at a level that is right for them. If the level of challenge is too low, children may become bored and 'switch off' from the learning experience. If the challenge is too great, they will struggle to achieve, with

failure as a likely outcome. With regard to spelling, it is vitally important to set activities at the right level of challenge to encourage success.

2. *Responding to pupils' diverse learning needs*...includes the need to:

- Create effective learning environments for all children.
- Secure (pupils') motivation and concentration.
- Provide equal opportunities for all learners.
- Ensure that assessment tasks are appropriate for all learners.
- Ensure that targets for learning are matched to individual needs.

Responding to pupils' diverse learning needs has implications for addressing different learning styles. This is particularly important for spelling. Some children may learn best through a **visual approach**. Others may struggle with visual spelling because they have poor memory skills. Learning styles in relation to spelling are addressed later in the book.

3. *Overcoming potential barriers to learning and assessment* for individuals and groups of pupils goes far beyond statements 1 and 2 above. A significant number of pupils with a **learning difficulty** or other form of **special educational need** may also require specialised equipment in order to access learning experiences. Pupils with a hearing impairment may need a radio aid to be worn by the adult who is teaching/supporting them. Children with a visual impairment may require materials with an enlarged font. Children with a language difficulty may require specific explanations or instructions that will help to eliminate any lack of language skills as a barrier to learning.

Children with learning difficulties may already be supported by **external specialists** as referred to in the *Revised Code of Practice for Special Educational Needs* (DfES 2001). This part of the inclusion statement refers to the specific action on behalf of schools that is intended to provide access for pupils with all kinds of learning difficulties in order to ensure their full participation in the National Curriculum.

Spelling is a major barrier to learning to write. For many children, motivation and confidence, once lost, can never be recovered. Therefore, *how* all adults support spelling is crucial to success. The following sections offer a brief introduction to spelling as part of the National Curriculum and the NLS as preparation for the rest of the book.

Spelling in the National Curriculum

Objectives for Key Stage 1 spelling and handwriting are summarised in the boxes below. For each objective, some strategies and resources for supporting these are suggested within further chapters.

Spelling in Key Stage 1

Children should be taught to:

- Write each letter of the alphabet.
- Use knowledge of **sound–symbol relationships** and **phonological patterns**.
- Recognise and use simple spelling patterns.
- Write common **letter strings**.
- Spell common words.
- Spell words with common **prefixes** and **inflectional endings**.
- Check accuracy of spelling using word banks and dictionaries.
- Use their knowledge of word families and other words.
- Identify reasons for misspelling.

Handwriting in Key Stage 1

Pupils should be taught:

- How to hold a pencil or pen.
- To write from left to right.
- To start and finish each letter correctly.
- To form letters of regular size and shape.
- To put regular spaces between words.
- To form **upper case letters**.
- How to join letters.

The above objectives aim to secure the basics of spelling and handwriting before children progress to Key Stage 2 and to facilitate further spelling development.

Now let's consider some objectives for spelling and handwriting at Key Stage 2, listed in the boxes below.

Spelling in Key Stage 2

Pupils should be taught to:

- Sound out **phonemes**.
- Analyse words into **syllables** and other known words.
- Apply knowledge of spelling conventions.
- Use knowledge of letter strings, visual patterns and **analogies**.
- Check spellings using word banks, dictionaries and spell checkers.
- Revise and build on knowledge of words and spelling patterns.

For morphology (study of word forms and systems) children should be taught:

- The meaning, use and spelling of common prefixes and **suffixes**.
- Spellings of words with inflectional endings.
- Relevance of word families, roots and origins of words.
- Use of appropriate terminology including **vowel**, **consonant**, **homophone** and **syllable**.

Handwriting in Key Stage 2

Children should be taught to:

- Write legibly...with increasing fluency and speed.
- Use different forms of handwriting for different purposes (e.g. labelling diagrams and notes).

Progression and skill acquisition

The National Curriculum sets out broad expectations for all children. But as we know, many have not secured all the objectives for Key Stage 1 by the time they move into Key Stage 2. It is crucial that spelling and handwriting skills are developed from the point which children have reached. I firmly believe that, as far as possible, each level of skills and knowledge must build on from the previous one.

While in practice most children may be working on the class-based objectives stated for a particular year or term, and are highly likely to 'catch on' to *some* of the skills and knowledge taught as they work, it is also vital that any gaps in previous learning are continually and urgently addressed if all children are to achieve according to their levels of expectation.

Certain areas of learning do need to be taught in the appropriate sequence. For example, we would not try to teach children how to sound out phonemes (sounds of letters) within words without first ensuring that their knowledge of individual letters is secure.

Spelling within the NLS

The NLS (now part of the Primary Strategy) drives the spelling curriculum in most schools. The literacy objectives operate on three levels: **word**, **sentence** and **text**. Although listed separately in the NLS framework (NLS 2001), all three levels need to be interlinked at the point of teaching and supporting any aspect of literacy. The spelling objectives appear under 'word level' and form the focus of this book.

Summary

In this chapter I have looked at:

- The National Curriculum statements of inclusion.
- The requirements of the National Curriculum for spelling at Key Stages 1 and 2.
- Spelling from a teaching perspective.

Chapter 2

Developing spelling competence

This chapter:

- Considers spelling development from the learner's perspectives.
- Describes the phases through which all learners pass on their way to becoming independent spellers.

First, consider the following words. Two are wrongly spelt – can you identify them?

embarrass	liquefy	battalion	coliseum	broccoli
beige	weild	focusing	sacrilegious	accidentally
mischievous	hypocrisy	aquiesce	consensus	lovable
moccasin	supersede	weather	separate	shriek

(The answers are on page 109.) Don't worry if you struggled to identify the errors without looking in a dictionary or at the answers – the above words are difficult for many adults to spell. We often have to think hard about words with double consonants (does *embarrass* have two r's and two s's?). I always used to confuse *separate* by putting *e* in the middle instead of *a*. Spelling is very difficult for many adults, but if you did identify the two errors, well done! You are probably one of a minority of excellent adult spellers.

Let's consider how children might reach such an exalted level of spelling. Gentry (1987) identified five main phases of spelling development. Knowing what these are will help us to assess children's spelling and address individual difficulties as they arise. The five phases need to be understood in relation to the National Curriculum and NLS objectives so that our teaching and support can result in effective learning outcomes for all children.

While there is no *direct* correlation between each phase of spelling described below and the NLS objectives for teaching spelling, some approximate links are suggested.

Phase 1 – Preliminary/emergent spelling

As a general guide this phase links to the Reception word level objectives for teaching spelling, although a few children may still be at this stage well into Year 1. At this emergent stage the child is getting to grips with the idea that symbols represent language. The child:

- Knows that print carries different messages, for example, to congratulate (birthday card), to entertain (novel), to inform (DIY manual for mending the car or a recipe for baking a cake).
- Uses letter-like symbols to represent language. These may consist of squiggles and a variety of mixed shapes, straight and curved.
- May have included recognisable letter shapes sprinkled within the attempted words.
- Is beginning to grasp the purpose of writing.

The examples below each illustrate spelling at this preliminary phase.

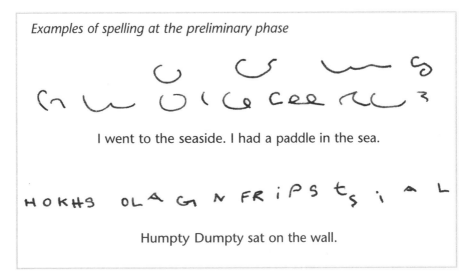

Examples of spelling at the preliminary phase

I went to the seaside. I had a paddle in the sea.

Humpty Dumpty sat on the wall.

As the examples illustrate, there is no one-to-one correspondence between the intended message and its written representation. A very brief message may be represented by more than half a page of writing or vice versa. The child is not fully aware that text prints from top to bottom and from left to right. Writing at this initial stage demonstrates very little in the way of spelling skills per se – the child is placing letters randomly rather than strategically to express meaning. What is important is that the child should assign a personal message to what is written and to tell an adult what it 'says'.

At this level, the child is aware that letters combine to form words and that words go together in writing, just as they do in speech. But these rather hesitant beginnings are important as they form the essential foundations for spelling.

How do we help the child to move on?

It is important that children know what 'words' and 'letters' mean. These concepts are often taken for granted. What is a word? Children need to realise that words:

- Can be of various lengths.
- May have one letter (a) or many letters (hippopotamus).
- May be on walls, on the white board, on cupboards or doors, on large sheets of paper as well as in their reading books (some children appear to think of words only as those in their reading books).
- Have different purposes either alone or within a phrase or sentence, for example, to label (on the pencils and rulers cupboard), to instruct or warn (poison, stop), or to question (why, how).

We can hardly encourage a child to put 'finger spaces' between attempted words if the concept of a word is not properly formed. Similarly, many children may only think of a letter as something the postman delivers with the mail.

Children at this preliminary phase need to begin to experience all kinds of print in order for these concepts to develop. What do letters and words actually do? What is their function in a book, a notice, a label and so on?

Children also need to experience this range of print in as many different fonts as possible: only by seeing slightly different forms and sizes of letters can children begin to grasp their distinguishing features in order to recognise them. The box below lists examples of the range and types of printed material that will help children to form early concepts of what writing is, as well as the function of the letters and words that constitute it.

What is writing?

Dictionaries / Restaurant menus / Telephone directory / Mobile phone instruction book / Magazines / Shopping lists / TV listings / Newspapers / Theatre programme / Leaflet for a safari park / Notice in the dentist/doctor's / Christmas present list / Novels / Non-fiction books / DIY manuals / Adverts / Passport / Driving licence / Road signs / Supermarket prices and adverts / Airport notices / Bus and train timetables / Diary / Text message on mobile / Letter from a friend (fast becoming a rare and valuable item) or an email

The list could be endless. All this range of print comes packaged in a variety of ways and forms part of the regular reading diet of most adults. Yet, even at the preliminary level, children need to form early concepts of the function of writing – the last thing we want is for children to think that 'writing' and 'spelling' is just 'what goes into their writing book'. At this preliminary phase, all children must start off with a positive concept of spelling. Chapter 4 details more specifically the objectives and strategies for developing spelling at the preliminary phase.

Phase 2 – Semi-phonetic spelling

This phase correlates loosely with how many children spell throughout Year 1 – some will still be at this level well into Year 2 – and builds onto the previous one in a number of ways as illustrated in the examples below.

Examples of spelling at the semi-phonetic phase

Frsd y6y

  H aft ta tak gLooW

  brys owt ov Tip

First you have to take glue–press out of top.

m favt t is sij ms a crts

My favourite tea is sausage, mash and carrots.

Children's spelling is likely to indicate:

- A greater awareness of print in general – the child may try to represent other types of writing format as well as prose.
- More consistent use of left to right and top to bottom orientation when writing in prose form.
- More strategic (rather than random) placing of letters within attempted words, for example, some correctly placed initial or end letters.
- Use of letters that are most obvious to the child himself. For example, the letters *s* and *t* are more easily identified as sounds within words than the letters *m* or *n*.

At this stage there is evidence of some letter–sound correspondence even though some sounds are omitted (*rds* for *rides*, or *cts* for *carrots*).

How do we help the child to move on?

Learners at this phase need to:

- Continue to develop their **phonological awareness** in a way that is soundly linked to the **phonic knowledge** that is taught from Reception and continued throughout Years 1 and 2. Many children move through these important years acquiring a great deal of phonic knowledge, but without having grasped the essential principles of spelling, for example, the notion of 'beginnings, middles and ends' (BME principle) in words without which phonic knowledge cannot be used effectively for spelling.

- Develop **rhyming** skills (*hat, cat, mat,* or *peach, teach, beach*). Many children fail to understand the notion of rhyme as words that have the same middle and end sound, but can be spelled differently, for example, *head, said* and *bed.* In poetry, such words are acceptable of course in relation to 'rhyme', but for the purpose of spelling we are seeking to develop the notion of rhyme as words that also have the same spellings.

A brief mention here about **onset and rime** that is not the same as rhyme. In this context, the onset refers to the first **grapheme**, while the rime refers to the rest of the word. Some examples of onset and rime are shown below.

Examples of onset and rime	
Same onset, with different rimes:	sheep, shin, ship, shoot (*sh* is the onset)
	lift, laugh, look, leaf (*l* is the onset)
Different onset, same rime	brawn, drawn, sawn (*awn* is the rime)
	shoot, boot, hoot (*oot* is the rime)

Note that the onset is often regarded as the first phoneme in a word with the rest of the word as the rime, but I prefer to keep double consonant clusters together, particularly in the early stages of learning to spell. So, in this context, *br* as in *brawn* is the onset; the rest of the word is the rime. The children must continue to try to spell new words as this offers opportunities to experiment and to use knowledge already gained.

Children at this stage are ready to develop their awareness of the difference between the **phonetic** and **visual** approaches to spelling to which I have already referred. Progress will be enhanced if they are taught to use the visual approach for learning the NLS 'tricky' words (e.g. *said, come, your*), alongside the phonetic approach for spelling unfamiliar words by hearing component sounds. Both strands need to be developed alongside each other although most children will tend to develop the phonetic strand first.

Also during this phase, children begin to develop what may become deep-rooted attitudes and thought processes for spelling (as well as hand-writing). Some of these may need adult intervention and guidance in order to prevent wrong attitudes from developing. For example, many children will try to **sound out** every word and need to be taught that some words need to be visually learned (more on this in further chapters).

Children at the semi-phonetic phase should have enough phonic know-ledge to start to talk about spelling. Such talk needs to be sensitive and positive in order to encourage the right attitudes towards spelling and to help all children to retain that healthy motivation they started out with, whatever their individual pace of development.

Now is the time to encourage young learners to think about spelling and to look at their own spellings at every opportunity. Chapter 5 explores the objectives and strategies that will help to move semi-phonetic spellers on to the next phase.

Phase 3 – Phonetic spelling

This phase correlates very loosely with how many children still spell throughout Year 2 and into Year 3, although some children in Year 2 will be much further on than this. Phonetic spelling is characterised by a more *strategic* placing of the correct letters on the basis of sound, as illustrated by the examples below. At this stage, most sounds in words are represented though not necessarily correctly (e.g. *cum* and *sed*).

Examples of spelling at the phonetic phase

I've
Iv got a Busey. it is Blue and Wayt [white]
stays   room
It stas in my livin rume. my
brother   share I've   called
Bruvr and me sher. Iv cald
it BoB

> the anjull cums to tell diffrint pipl
> (angel) (cums) (people)
> that thay haf To ASciyp wayl herad
> (escape) (while) (Herod)
> wosnt Wochin
> (watching)

Most attempted words would now be decipherable within the context of a piece of writing as are many of the attempted words in the above examples. Also, syllables in longer words are starting to be represented more efficiently, for example, *wicend* for 'weekend' or *roodolf* for 'Rudolph'.

Most of the sounds are represented in the correct sequence. The letter clusters may not be correct, but they are logical and representative of the English language. On the whole, they represent how words *could* be spelled, for example, *leeph* (leaf), *flore* (floor). This spelling illustrates the learner's growing knowledge of **grapheme combinations** from which to choose when trying to spell an unfamiliar word.

How do we help the child to move on?

We need to continue to encourage experimental spelling using the phonic approach (listening to the sequential sounds in words). Alongside this, the child should be ready to develop the visual approach to spelling, using the **Look, Say, Cover, Write, Check (LSCWC)** strategy. When teaching these, emphasise to children that each approach serves a different purpose for spelling. We need to 'hear' unfamiliar words but 'see' in our minds the tricky words that do not follow a regular phonic pattern.

Phonetic spellers should now start to learn more of the rules and conventions that govern English spelling. For example, following the 'y to ie' rule – *cherry* and *berry* change to *cherries* and *berries* when there is more than one. Children also need to investigate word families in order to develop further their logical approach to thinking about the *most likely* choice when trying to spell an unfamiliar word. Investigating which groups of vowels and consonants form likely combinations will help to develop an experience of different groups. The choices are far from simple, for example, *beef, thief, leaf.* Which vowel digraph (e.g. *ee, ea* or *ie*) would you choose in order to spell *chief* if that word was completely new to you? After all, given the many irregularities of English, *cheef* or *cheaf* would seem a sensible choice to many learners.

Children at this stage also need to develop their awareness and understanding of syllables, building on from their growing ability to represent these in their spelling. Working on common prefixes and suffixes will help to develop an understanding of how syllables are formed.

Phonetic spellers also need to talk about words. More discussion will encourage the logical choices that distinguish sensible spelling attempts from those that cannot be correct. For example, learners need to know that consonants must be separated by vowels and at a higher level, that prefixes are always placed at the beginning of words. What is obvious to us may not be as obvious to learners as the totally illogical examples shown below may illustrate.

Prefix and suffix non-words and words with no vowels	
ed / vite / in	phs
ent / depend / in	tchr
ci / de / sion	crrct
stant / sub / ial	lttr
chant / en / ing	phnm

No doubt, you correctly sequenced the prefix and suffix words with ease and identified the words without vowels as *phase, teacher, correct, letter* and *phoneme.* Why is it that we can read the above words without the vowels? For most of us, these words form part of our reading and spelling experiences, i.e. we simply *know* them.

This type of activity would help to develop prefix and suffix knowledge. Ask children to form sensible words by placing the parts in the correct sequence, but make sure that they know and understand the prefixes and suffixes used in the activities. The development of logical thinking about spelling is crucial to success and accompanies the planned and word-specific phonic teaching.

At this stage, playing with **non-words** also helps to develop phonological awareness to more sophisticated levels. Most learners enjoy working with non-words as they know that there can be no *correct* version and, therefore, no failure. Discussions with non-words merely focus on what is sensible and logical in relation to what children already know about spelling conventions.

For example, if children are learning to **segment** letter sounds to spell **consonant-vowel-consonant** (CVC) words (*rat, pin, hat*), practising with non-words helps them to use their phonic skills for any CVC combination – *rab, hon, pib*. With non-words, the focus is also on the accuracy of the phonic skills per se rather than on their growing recognition of common words.

Phonological awareness is often perceived to be a necessary precedent to phonic knowledge. In one sense it is, particularly at the early stages, but it is also important that a learner's phonological awareness should develop alongside phonic knowledge. Even when children are being taught prefixes and suffixes (*un, dis, sion, ment*), or the long vowel sounds (*ea, oo, oi, ow*), their phonological understanding of how to think about and use acquired phonic skills needs to be continued. Chapter 6 explores some objectives and strategies for developing spelling throughout Key Stage 2 which will help to move learners on to the next stage.

Phase 4 – Transitional spelling

This stage correlates loosely with the NLS spelling objectives to be secured throughout Key Stage 2. While attainment in spelling by now will be very widely spread, and some children will still be at the semi-phonetic or the phonetic phase of spelling, those who have reached the transitional phase will represent all of the consonant and vowel sounds in their spelling, even if they are not always correct. There will generally be at least one vowel in every syllable as the child now demonstrates knowledge of common letter patterns and knows a lot about English spelling conventions.

Every syllable must have at least one vowel

A   me   hat   reach   spelling   protection   development
Help – where are my *vwls*?

(NB: Of course, this is English we are talking about and there are exceptions, e.g. my.)

The visual approaches to spelling should now be well developed and learners should know how to apply either approach (visual, phonic or both strategies combined) to suit their own spelling purpose.

By this stage, the learner will be able to recognise many words and there should be a greater reliance on visual clues. Those children who are on track with their spelling will, by the end of Year 4, be able to spell all or most of the tricky words from the NLS list and this knowledge will be used sensibly to inform other spelling attempts.

How do we help the child to move on?

Learners continue to need exposure to a range of print experience with opportunities to talk about all aspects of language. Indeed, talking about spelling within the context of language helps to retain the motivation and enthusiasm with which our learners started out. Talking about spelling problems in a sensitive and enjoyable way will keep learners on board and help to prevent them from opting out of the learning experience. Sadly, talk is something that is often neglected as the NLS objectives for reading and writing are rigorously pursued. While there is little time to fit every-thing in, teaching assistants can perhaps help children to build onto the formal lessons on spelling and develop their *thinking* through positive and well-focused talk.

Specifically, learners at this transitional phase need to develop their knowledge of language patterns and their interrelationships. Work on spelling should now be linked with a growing understanding of **grammar** and the history of the English language from which spellings are derived. These learners are ready to study the grammatical elements of English within the context of spelling. For example, how do we formulate a noun into an adjective (familiarity into familiar) or change an adjective into an adverb (quick into quickly)? What meaning do you conjure up from a colleague's self-described 'Mozartian moment'?

Children now need to develop their proficiency in *applying* their exten-sive knowledge of common letter strings and patterns. This is why spelling must now be linked to grammar work in order to give it meaning. Nothing will destroy all that hard work and fought-for enthusiasm more quickly than meaningless spelling work, focusing on parts of words, if children do not understand where the parts fit into the whole. The example below illustrates spelling at the transitional phase.

Examples of spelling at the transitional phase

Our body

Bones are joined together to make a skeliton. When you grase your self blood comes out. If you touch something it feels soft smooth silky rouf and prickly. In the middel of your eye is a pupul that is what you see with.

The Race

I looked over my strolder and suddanly [shoulder] [suddenly]
realised the other bikers were catching me up.
I toke over them in good stile. They had
made a big mistake letting me past. Then
I hit the flor. [floor]

Phase 5 – Independent spelling

By the end of Year 4 or into Year 5, some 'good' spellers will be well on their way to developing their independence, while others may still be lingering at the transitional or earlier phases. Children who have reached the independent phase have acquired almost all of the rules and conventions and are using multi-strategic approaches towards spelling that is mainly correct as illustrated below. These spellers are able to visualise through their mind's eye from a large repertoire of known words, as you probably did when you tried to identify the two errors from the list of difficult words at the start of this chapter.

A significant feature of this final phase is the learner's ability to take responsibility for further development. These learners will identify their errors and put them right. They will find out what they need to know and should no longer be dependent on adults for information. They will continue to learn about interrelationships between words through grammar work and should be able to link this to spelling development.

Examples of spelling at the independent phase

> The lion who wanted to ride a motorbike
>
> A lion wanted to ride on a motorbike. The other lions said "we cant ride motorbikes as we are made for fighting other animals .... Birds cant ride motorbikes they are for flying and whistlig in trees. The lion saw Tom's bike. It was roaring and looked exsiting. ...... When the bike stoped the lion said "that was to scary."

Part of this work on the interrelationships between words will take place more extensively across the curriculum as children acquire more subject-specific vocabulary in science, history, geography, art and so on. Spelling should continue to be part of the work done within the subject context; subject specialists in secondary schools are just as responsible for spelling *within their subject* as staff in the English and learning support departments.

In summary, although there is no *direct* correlation, the phases which the majority of children progress through in order to become competent and independent spellers often relate to the NLS objectives for year groups as shown in the box below. More competent spellers will progress far more quickly than this and may have reached the transitional phase by the end of Year 2. Conversely, those who find spelling extremely difficult may still be at the semi-phonetic phase as they enter Year 4. The chart offers loose pegs on which to hang pupil expectations, but care must be taken not to have exactly the same rigid expectations for all learners without due regard to their individual styles and paces of learning. Many children will not be able to match NLS expectations. Attempting to teach later skills and knowledge before children are ready will only cause confusion and severely limit the progress towards spelling competency rather than enhance it.

Links between learning phases and NLS expectations

Learning phase	NLS objective for year group
Phase 1 Preliminary spelling	Reception
Phase 2 Semi-phonetic spelling	Throughout Year 1
Phase 3 Phonetic spelling	Throughout Year 2
Phase 4 Transitional spelling	Throughout Years 3 to 4
Phase 5 Independent spelling	Year 5 onwards

Furthermore, progression in spelling is often far from evenly balanced. Some children may develop their visual spelling strengths but struggle to develop phonic skills, while others progress the other way round. For example, some children with good memories may be better able to retain tricky words visually but will struggle to develop phonic knowledge because of poor phonological awareness.

Paying attention to spelling development on an individual basis is essential if children are to develop different strategies at the same time. Some children may also need more intensive reinforcement of the key concepts at any particular phase in order to keep up with a spelling programme. Furthermore, many children may not show consistency in their spelling. The need to rush through a piece of writing without adequate time for redrafting, as often happens in the literacy hour, may result in pieces of writing by the same child that show considerable variation in spelling quality.

Summary

In this chapter I have looked at:

- The five phases of spelling: preliminary, semi-phonetic, phonetic, transitional and independent.
- How we can help children to move on from each of these phases to become independent spellers.

Chapter 3

Principles for supporting spelling

Having considered the teaching requirements for spelling in Chapter 1 and the learner's journey towards independent spelling in Chapter 2, this chapter considers some essential principles for supporting spelling that will help to ensure success.

The NLS objectives are hugely demanding and based on an assumption that all children are ready for intensive work on spelling (and other areas of literacy) from the beginning of schooling. Secondly, and more of a potential barrier to success for some learners, is the focus on getting through the objectives at a brisk pace with few opportunities for any necessary reinforcement, for example, on letter formation. In many schools, the rush to cover the NLS objectives for the term overshadows many important principles for teaching that help to provide a positive 'learning to spell' experience. Paying some attention to the principles of teaching spelling can go a long way towards eliminating potential barriers.

As a child how did you learn to spell? Can you remember the strategies you were taught at school or is the whole experience lost in the distant past? More importantly, do you recall your experiences of learning how to spell as positive or negative in the way they affected your self-esteem? These are important questions for our learners. Being able or not able to spell within the context of writing can greatly affect children's self-esteem.

So, alongside the National Curriculum and NLS requirements, what principles do we need to apply to our support for spelling? Let's look at this from the learner's perspective. Apart from the backbone of specifically taught phonic knowledge, spelling development also relies on:

● Efficient memory – to retain what is taught.

- Language acquisition – a range of vocabulary and the knowledge of grammar within which spelling is embedded (especially at Key Stage 2).
- **Visual discrimination** skills.
- **Auditory discrimination** skills.
- Phonological awareness.
- Ability to retain skills and knowledge, and to generalise what is known across the curriculum.
- Children's ability to maximise their personal learning styles.
- A learner's confidence to try new words with the awareness that spelling is a long-term developmental process.
- Regular perceptions of success to spur learners on.
- A sensitive and fun-based learning experience.
- Awareness of children's strengths and weaknesses.
- Trust in the adults who are guiding their learning.
- Awareness that the process comes before the product.

Let's explore some of these principles.

▨ Training memory

Professionals often refer to children as having either 'good' or 'poor' memories, but rarely are children trained to develop their memories for learning purposes. In the box below are a number of shapes. Try looking at them for ten seconds before covering them up. How many large circles? How many small ones? How many squares? How many triangles altogether and how many of these are right-angled triangles?

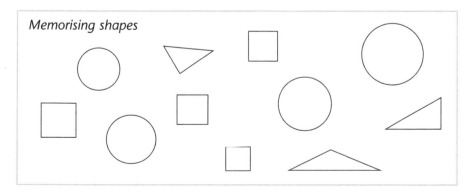

Memorising shapes

It's a bit like the memory game on TV (*The Generation Game*) in which contestants recalled items that passed by on a conveyor belt. If they recalled all the items, did they recall them in the same order?

When children look at a word in order to learn it, we expect them to 'see' the word clearly, to create the right **perception** of what the eye takes in (pass it to the brain) and hence to memorise it. They need to take in the overall shape of a word as well as its significant features. How would you try to memorise the non-words in the box below?

Memorising non-words

| inchantion | entimed | repriment | subleating |
| trendingment | disleadial | intercheepen | imploosing |

Some of the words may not even be logical as English spellings, but what strategies did you employ to try to memorise them? Did you apply your knowledge of prefixes and suffixes? Did you chunk the longer words (split each one into syllables)? Did you try to memorise significant letter strings? There are no right or wrong ways to memorise words – each of us has our own way of trying to learn them.

From the start of schooling, there is a strong emphasis on children learning how to spell the so-called tricky words from the NLS lists. Without an adequate memory this cannot be successful. The following activities could help to develop children's memories:

- Variation on 'Kim's game' – show a child a number of objects on a tray then take one (or two) away. Use toys, objects, numbers or letters. Can the child recall the missing items?

- Show the child a word. Ask him/her to look at it and try to remember all the letters. Then take away a letter. Can the child say which letter has gone? This is particularly effective with tricky words such as *they* (focus on the *e*) or *said* (focus on the *ai*). Vary this from single letters removed to letter strings, depending on the level the child is working on (e.g. you might remove the *ea* in *peach* or *str* in *string*).

- Memorising from dictation – ask the child to write letters (or numbers) from dictation. Start with only two or three and progress to six, seven or more as the child's confidence increases. Vary the difficulty by asking the child to recall and reorganise at the same time, for example, putting numbers in numerical rather than random order or letters into alphabetical order.

● Focus on meaning – most information is assigned to our memories alongside some meaningful strategy for retaining it. Learning involves making sense of pieces of information and committing them to our memory's long-term 'filing system'. We may file it with other items in a category. For example, to learn the word *they* we might place it with other words which have the word 'the' inside, such as *them, then, there*. To learn the word *should* we might place it with other words in the same rhyming family (*would* and *could*). It is important for each learner to memorise words according to his own learning style.

● **Mnemonics** and **acronyms** – one child in my class, when asked to spell the word 'said', always recited aloud 'Sally Ann is dancing'. Other mnemonics often help children to remember particular words: 'Big elephants can always use small exits' is a favourite for the word 'because'. Personally, I prefer a visual strategy as I can never remember the mnemonic in order to assign it to the spelling, but if this is an effective aid to memory for some children, then we need to help them use it.

● Avoid copying – never allow a child to copy words letter by letter as he/she does not have to remember anything. Make memory a need and it will develop. When asked for the spelling of a word, ask the child to offer one or more letters, depending on the phase reached. Then write down the word and ask the child to study it before using the LSCWC strategy to spell it.

▨ Language acquisition

There is little point in trying to teach children to spell words they neither understand nor use as part of their spoken language. The problem with the (tricky) **high-frequency words** from the NLS lists is that they have no intrinsic meaning and can only be understood as part of a phrase or sentence.

Can you form an image in your mind of the words *in italics only* from the box below in isolation? It is highly unlikely that you can. Without the meaning-carrying words that accompany these, such as *boat, beach, six, dog, cat, fish* and *chips*, there is no inherent meaning.

> *High-frequency words have little intrinsic meaning*
>
> *In the* boat. / *On the* beach. / *About* six o'clock. / *The* dog chased *the* cat. / *They* went *for some* fish *and* chips.

Children whose language is delayed, when they arrive at school tend not to know many of the high-frequency words so these need to be discussed and presented within a meaningful context, and always within a sentence.

At a more sophisticated level, the spelling of subject-specific words may be difficult if they are not properly understood. What do you understand by the word 'photosynthesis'? If you do not know what it means (as many of us may not), and cannot chunk its parts, how can you remember its spelling? It is important to ensure, when working on the spelling of subject-based words, that children have grasped their meanings. This principle applies especially in Key Stage 2 with the emphasis on grammar. Children whose language is limited to that of school, home and the local community may need to be sensitively taught **Standard English** alongside their spelling programme.

▨ Visual discrimination skills

How good are you at distinguishing visual differences? This is a learned skill. Children need to start with broad differences, for example, of colour or mathematical shapes. They soon learn to recognise the attributes which make each shape different: that circles are formed from one continuous, curved line, while triangles have three straight lines and three points. Gradually children need to refine their visual skills to appreciate smaller differences, for example, between letters. Many letters are different only in minor details, as illustrated below, especially the handwritten versions.

Differences in letter shapes					
hn	gy	bdp	ao	oc	ce
ij	ft	un	wm	mn	hb

Study each pair of letters and visualise their handwritten versions. How are they different? Most letters differ only in one tiny feature, for example, in size, orientation or some tiny detail that may be only apparent when the letter is *perfectly written*. What does a handwritten *g* look like if the top is not closed together? What does the *h* look like without its **ascender**? Children should consider these questions as part of their work on letter learning to help them to notice minor details that distinguish one letter from another.

Phonological awareness and auditory discrimination

Each of these terms refers to the ability to hear and to identify sounds within words in the right order. When trying to spell an unfamiliar word we rely on:

● Hearing the word.

● Segmenting each phoneme within the word.

● Recognising each phoneme in sequence within the word.

● Matching each phoneme to its grapheme in order to spell the word.

Children must distinguish between different everyday sounds before they can start to develop phonological awareness, for example, a dog barking, the doorbell, the ping of the microwave, a human voice. Such broad differences then become refined as children distinguish between different voices and assign a voice to a person.

Phonological awareness develops in a similar way from the broad to the refined. Children need to hear and to recognise different sounds within words at the level of the most minute detail, for example, the difference between *rob* and *rub* or the difference between *ship* and *chip*. They also need to hear and recognise sounds such as *fr* in *frog* as different from *fl* in *flog*. Similarly, recognition of the vowel differences in words such as *strong*, *string* and *strung* may rely on clear speech and language context.

In addition, many children struggle to distinguish between some 'softer' or similar sounds, for example, between *m* and *n*, *b* and *p*, or even between *s* and *z*. The pronunciation as well as the spelling of words containing *th* is notoriously difficult for some children and is often represented when spelling as *f*. Phonological awareness also depends on an awareness of sounds in their sequence. Even if children do recognise most of the sounds referred to above, they may not do so in the right order to support spelling.

The concept of sounds occurring at the beginning, middle and end of words is a crucial principle without which spelling is a non-starter. This notion starts with the blending or segmentation of single letter sounds and develops as a cumulative set of ideas as spelling knowledge progresses. Even words with prefixes and suffixes have an identifiable beginning, middle and end, as we can see from the examples below. Learners who are taught to think about this concept will have a head start towards success.

Beginnings, middles and ends of words

Progression level	Beginning	Middle	End
Single letters	m	a	t
Initial clusters	cr	o	p
End clusters	p	a	st
Long vowel sounds	b	ea	ch
	sh	oo	t
	bl	oa	t
	sp	oi	l
	str	a	p
Prefix and suffix	en	chant	ment
	dis	integrate	ed

When trying to spell words with prefixes and suffixes, our thoughts may focus on identifying the *root* of a word, which is often in the middle (integrate) and to which the prefix and suffix are 'attached' (dis...ed). By this stage of thinking about spelling, working with prefixes and suffixes depends largely on accurate identification of the syllables within roots of words (*integrate* has three). So, if we attempt to spell the word *disintegrated,* we may identify three syllables within its root plus a prefix and a suffix. Phonological processing may start simply, but becomes more complex as spelling work develops.

Skill mastery and generalising known knowledge across the curriculum

If we want children to generalise their skills and to use them in other contexts in order to support further learning, then those skills need to be thoroughly mastered. For example, we should try to ensure that individual letters are secured before we ask children to segment words into sounds in order to spell them. Similarly, if a child is still struggling to spell at CVC level (*hat, pin, rub*) we should try to secure these before teaching the consonant clusters (*crab, snip*) or long vowels sounds (b*ee*p, h*au*l, sp*oi*l). The box below offers a sequence of phonic development that is roughly compatible with the NLS objectives for teaching spelling.

Sequence of phonic progression

CVC three-letter words	pan, hen, sit, dog, rub
CVC four-letter words	buff, sell, fizz, mess (ff, ll, zz, ss)
	sick, peck, lock (ck)
	ship, thin, chip (sh, th, ch)

(NB: Stress the CVC components of these words when teaching.)

Initial double consonant clusters (CCVC)	blot, crab, flip, frog, glum
(CCVCC)	black, grass, brick, swill, shock
Initial triple consonant clusters	strap, spring, split, thrill
Final double consonant clusters (CVCC)	hand, milk, bank, hunt, cold
Above in longer words and with plural forms	splendid, stripping
Words with long vowel phonemes	leek (ee), pain (ai), chief (ie), coat (oa), food (oo)

Endings	ing, es, ed, as in thrilling, buses, milked
More vowel phonemes	oo (as in good), ar (car), ow (cow, low), oy (boy)
Other common spellings	air (hair), or (port), er (tiger), split vowels a–e (as in rate, time, home), ph (phase), Ch (Christmas)
Compound words	postman, himself, pancake
Prefixes and suffixes	un, dis, de, in, sion, ment, as part of syllable and grammar work

The above list is not intended as a complete list of phonic patterns, more as a guide for teaching and practice purposes.

It is important to remember that even if children have not secured each level of spelling along the way, learning should not stop – whatever the challenge, most children will still manage to catch on to various elements of learning as they progress and later on will often produce the evidence when we least expect it, all of which is wonderfully surprising.

On the other hand, if we want children to transfer and to practise their spelling skills in other contexts they must have grasped the key points. Common to most children with learning difficulties is their inability to generalise learning and to use it to support further learning. Many children need explicit help to do this.

Differences in pupils' learning styles

The National Curriculum statement for inclusion invites us to celebrate diversity. All of us learn in different ways and there are many ways of thinking about learning styles. The differences in learning styles identified by Given and Reid (1999) and illustrated below is one simple way of considering how different children may learn.

Differences in learning styles

Emotional	Places human emotions as the driving force of learning and promotes interest, motivation, responsibility and persistence on the part of the learner.
Social	Needing (or not) to relate to others while learning.
Cognitive	How the brain makes sense of learning situations and satisfies the logical 'need to know' element.
Physical	Based on the need to do, to move and to be active while learning.
Reflective	Based on individual responses to learning situations with the emphasis on thinking through as the basic learning strategy.

What do learning styles have to do with spelling? Clearly, our emotions influence our success and promote a sense of responsibility and eventual independence, so all learners need to enjoy their spelling activities. **Social learners** will enjoy working in groups, but not all children like to learn in groups all the time – there may be times when some prefer to work alone. **Cognitive learners** will need to know in advance what they are to learn and why. I consider myself a cognitive learner – whenever I attend a course, I like to know in advance what the learning objectives are for the session. **Physical learners** prefer to move around the classroom. They like to go to the front of the class and hold up a letter card or hold up words and wave their hands about at their desks. **Reflective learners** may not have an answer straight away; they may think deeply before they respond and need time for tasks and activities (I also fall partly into this category).

How do you learn best? The point of knowing about learning styles is not so that we can try to match a particular style to each learner and reflect this for every task. Whatever our favoured learning style, all of us are, to some extent, composites of the above styles, depending on what we are learning. While it is useful to identify a learner's particular style, if, over time, spelling work features a range of activities that reflect each of the learning styles listed above, this should help to ensure learning for all. Having said that, we do need to identify how children learn spellings best, especially at a point when some begin to demonstrate spelling difficulties.

For example, Stevie has an excellent memory. He can remember the tricky words with no problem, but he struggles with phonic work and needs to be coached carefully in this area. Memory as a sole strategy for spelling will not sustain long-term success. Fiona, on the other hand, struggles to learn the high-frequency words because her visual skills are weak. She learns best when there is a strong emphasis on meaning, for example, through mnemonics.

Developing spelling confidence

Children need to perceive spelling as a developmental process that will continue throughout most of their time in school – and later than that for some less able spellers. Those who perceive spelling work throughout school as a kind of apprenticeship, and expect to develop their skills gradually, over time, are more likely to enjoy the process. Those learners who expect to 'get it right' from the beginning are likely to be anxious. Spelling work should never breed anxiety.

What would be a sensitive learning environment for spelling? Consider the following attributes:

- *Having a go*: 'Have-a-go' spellers are confident in the knowledge that they are unlikely to spell an unfamiliar word right the first time they try. They almost expect to get it partly wrong in order to get it right later. It is the consistency of 'trying' that eventually achieves success.

- *Right or wrong*: These confident spellers also know that there is no 'right' or 'wrong' during the process of learning to spell. From the start, any concept of wrongness puts up a barrier to success that less confident spellers can do without. From the learners' perspective, spellings must always be 'somewhere along the road to rightness'. They must be able to see some progression. The worst thing adults can do is to correct every attempt. If a child spells the word *rides* as *rds*, this means that three out of five letters are correct. Wonderful! Know what is expected from each child's attempts. Is it just the initial letter for children at the earliest phase? Or should the child be able to identify the long vowel *au* as it was taught last week? The child who spells *magic* as *machick* is recognising syllables within words and needs praise for such efforts.

While we should have challenging but realistic expectations for all learners, within these parameters we need to remain sensitive to the principle of having a go without placing undue emphasis on right or wrong.

Promoting success

The development of competence also relies on children's perceptions of their success. Those learners who consider themselves as 'failures' early on in the process will soon lose any motivation to try. Issues such as those outlined above, for example, having a go and the sensitive approaches to spellings as 'partly right', will all help to improve children's perceptions of themselves as spellers who are progressing through a lengthy process as well as helping to boost self-esteem in general.

Children also need to know that they are only competing against themselves. Personal success can be measured against what was achieved yesterday, last week or even the previous term, but never against the achievements of other children.

Let's enjoy learning to spell!

All learning should be enjoyable and spelling is one of the most difficult areas of learning in which children can achieve success. Laughter supports learning, but it often seems as if the enjoyment declines beyond Key Stage 1. The government document *Excellence and Enjoyment* (DfES 2003) emphasises the role of enjoyment in learning throughout school.

Clearly, we cannot play games all of the time and we would not want the emphasis on fun to detract from the serious business of learning. On the other hand, most spelling activities can incorporate a fun element somewhere, and by encouraging children to laugh and learn throughout the spelling process we will reduce much of the anxiety that often accompanies work on spelling. Some suggestions for enjoyable activities are featured in the following chapters.

Trust

If children are to have faith in themselves as spellers and in their own progression, they must trust the adults who are guiding them. We can help children to trust through being consistent in our responses to their spelling efforts and by explaining the reasons for our decisions. Children need to know that adults care about their learning (and their well-being). Once trust is established, children will be happy to talk about themselves in the context of learning. Positive and focused talk (about spelling or other areas of learning) will help to remove any barriers as soon as they start to emerge. All children should be fully involved in their learning process and this issue is explored in Chapter 7.

Process before product

Confidence in spelling is enhanced by the effectiveness of the learning environment. What children see around them influences their attitudes and perceptions of spelling. So why is it that much of the time, especially as parents' evenings approach, classroom walls become covered with 'perfect' examples of children's writing (and spelling)? If some of this space could be reserved for work that shows the process, for example, crossings out and amended spellings, both children and parents would appreciate the importance of putting the learning process before the end product. Seeing at first hand the initial drafts that have preceded each finished piece would remind all of us to value the time and effort that has gone into the polished work.

The challenge of knowing our learners

Children's confidence in learning to spell comes partly from knowing that progress is being made, however slowly. Each small indication of success, often rewarded with a 'well-done' sticker or praise alone, places another secure brick in the achievement wall. Such security stems from having suitable challenges to achieve.

As adults, most of us have experienced times when we have been required to do something that *we have felt* was beyond us. At times our own challenges are seen as too high or even insurmountable. But being challenged does help to keep us on our toes and to realise our potential and personal aspirations. Like adults, children will respond in different ways, either by rising to the challenge and striving to do their best or by feeling that they can't possibly achieve it anyway and therefore not bothering to try. So, with regard to spelling, how can we help children to rise to their challenges and to achieve their best? The trick is to know the learner! Being aware of each child's strengths and weaknesses will enable us to present suitable and realistic challenges for spelling.

What do we mean by challenge? Targets that are too easy for individual learners are likely to ensure 'success' on their terms, but are unlikely to ensure progression. Conversely, presenting children with spelling tasks beyond their level is likely to produce feelings of failure. Targets for spelling need to be set at a level that makes children use the knowledge and skills they have already and at the same time take learning a step further. In terms of challenge, it is the *size of the next step* that is crucial to success. For one child, being able to spell all of the high-frequency words on the NLS list for Reception may be just right. For another, being able to spell half of these would be a more appropriate challenge for that term. Knowing the learners is crucial to setting suitably challenging targets for spelling.

Spelling as part of independent writing

The cliché 'use it or lose it' applies as much to spelling as it does to any other area of learning. For example, children cannot be expected to learn the tricky words from the NLS lists and to *retain them* unless they have plenty of opportunities for using them within their writing. All subjects offer opportunities for spelling reinforcement through cross-curricular work – even phonic knowledge taught in the literacy hour can be re-inforced through subject learning. For example, children will respond well to finding words in other subject areas that contain the vowel digraphs that they have been taught.

Throughout Key Stage 2 it is even more important, as subjects are further separated into discrete areas of learning, that grammar work should include subject-based vocabulary.

Summary

In this chapter I have looked at:

● The principles for spelling that underpin success and progress for all children. These need to be borne in mind throughout the rest of the book as we chart the objectives from the NLS that drive the spelling curriculum and explore some strategies for helping learners to achieve them.

Chapter 4

Developing spelling in the Reception year

This chapter correlates loosely with spelling progression from the preliminary to the semi-phonetic phase identified in Chapter 2. We will explore:

- Spelling objectives from the NLS for the Reception year.
- Strategies for teaching them.
- Early handwriting skills (letter formation).

The Reception year is an opportunity for children to be introduced to the principles of spelling as explored in the previous chapter. It is also expected that most learners will make a promising start to their spelling by acquiring the key skills listed below.

NLS objectives for the Reception year

By the end of the Reception year children need to:
- Understand **rhyme**.
- Match phonemes (sounds) to graphemes (letters) by:
  - identifying sounds in **CVC words** at the beginning and end
  - knowing the sounds for letters *sh*, *ch* and *th*, as well as *a–z*.
- Establish the beginnings of **alphabetic** and phonic knowledge, i.e.:
  - sounds and names of letters in both upper and lower case
  - alphabetical order.
- Link sounds to their spelling patterns by:
  - identifying families of rhyming words
  - recognising onsets and rimes
  - recognising **alliteration**.
- Recognise critical features of words (e.g. shape, length and common patterns).

Even in Reception, there is a great deal to be taught and many children enter Year 1 without having acquired these essential basics. Having 'fallen behind', these children then start to focus on the Year 1 spelling objectives at a significant disadvantage.

The reasons why children fall behind with their learning are not always linked to special educational needs – some are simply not ready to benefit from the experiences at the time they are offered. Many may have missed out on rich, language-based play experiences before school. Once delayed, language is a difficult area in which to catch up. Children may lack some or all of the following areas of spoken language:

- Vocabulary – even the common words to describe the home, school or local community.
- A range of sentence structures – for example, the language to describe past and future events. The inability to use verb structures in spoken language correctly is common at Reception level.
- Knowledge of the NLS high-frequency words that are featured throughout Key Stage 1 spelling work.

Listen to children talking among themselves in the playground as well as to adults and you immediately notice those who have not acquired the language skills they will need for learning. The companion book in this series, *Supporting Speaking and Listening*, contains a host of information and practical suggestions for helping children to develop their language skills.

A further group of children may lack the visual and auditory discrimination skills needed to develop phonological awareness. Children who enter Reception without the prerequisite skills that enable them to learn will be severely at risk perhaps throughout the rest of their school lives. Alongside a sensitive and rich learning environment, throughout which their development is carefully monitored, some children may also need an individualised intervention programme that operates in parallel with normal class-based work to help them to catch up.

Having emphasised the importance of ensuring that all children can benefit from the NLS work in Reception, let's look at how we might develop the objectives listed above.

Understanding rhyme

This objective requires children to:

- Explore rhyming patterns, for example, nursery rhymes.
- Through analogy, generate new and invented words.

Nursery rhymes offer children an introduction to the idea of rhyme long before they are expected to spell rhyming words. Have some of the nursery rhymes listed below remained in your memory since school?

> Mary, Mary, quite contrary, how does your garden grow?
> Georgie Peorgie pudding and pie, kissed the girls and made them cry
> Humpty Dumpty sat on a wall, Humpty Dumpty had a great fall
> Hey, diddle, diddle, the cat and the fiddle, the cow jumped over the moon

Can you continue with the lines of each rhyme? If so, why do you think this is? What benefit did you gain from nursery rhymes when you were at school? Did you always understand them? I certainly didn't – after all, few of them make any sense!

Nursery rhymes are fun, whether or not children understand them. And clearly singing rhymes is a strong memory aid. But what is their value in terms of learning to understand rhyme (for spelling)? What do children need to take from the 'singing' of them? I ask this question because some children take part in singing nursery rhymes and enjoy the activities, but emerge with little idea of what the rhymes are supposed to convey. They have simply missed the point. This may be because the notion of the *rhyme* itself has somehow become lost within the singing.

We can avoid this by drawing attention to the words that rhyme. Focus on hearing, not spelling, as the spelling patterns may not match. You might:

- Sing a few rhymes together.
- Explain to the children what rhyming is and pick out a few examples from the rhymes (*pie* and *cry*).
- Ask children to say clearly the words that rhyme.
- Ask them if the words sound the same at the beginning or at the end. It is important to establish this key principle of rhyming from the start.

- In order to generate new and invented words that rhyme, ask children to add new words that follow the same pattern, for example, from *pie* and *cry*, they may come up with *high*, *by*, *guy*, *lie* among others.
- Emphasise that it's what they sound like that matters.
- Throw in some odd words that don't fit the rhyming pattern and see if children can identify the odd one out. Why is it the odd one? Talk about the difference.

Once initial work on nursery rhymes has moved on to exploring words that rhyme, take children's thinking forward by identifying rhyming words that illustrate different sound patterns, for example, with consonants at the end – *stand, hand, sand, land,* or sets with long vowels – *grow, mow, sew, bow, foe.* It is a good idea to write these words down and let children see that the letters are not expected to match – this will allow them to appreciate that rhyme is solely to do with sound.

Some children may be able to invent their own rhymes based on the rhythms and patterns of those they have heard – the sillier, the better if they help children to appreciate the concept of rhyming.

Matching phonemes to graphemes

This is NLS speak for being able to match letter sounds with their shapes. The phoneme is the sound; the grapheme is the letter (or letters) that can represent each sound. To achieve this objective, children need to be able to:

- Hear and identify initial sounds in words.
- Write the letters that represent each sound.
- Identify initial and dominant phonemes in spoken words.
- Identify and write the initial and final phonemes in CVC words.

Let's see what it all means.

Hearing and identifying initial sounds in words

The initial sound in a word is the first sound, but this is not always matched to a single letter, for example, *sh*out, *ch*ips, *th*ump as compared with *t*eddy or *d*oll. At this stage, we want children to grasp the idea that sounds within words are in sequence (the principle of a beginning, middle and end), otherwise they will struggle to pick out the initial sound as the first one. It is better to introduce this idea with initial sounds that are single letters (*b*all in preference to *br*idge) rather than confuse children with those that are less easy to identify.

First, ensure that children can distinguish sounds in general (microwave pinging, dog barking, human voice). It may seem obvious, but it is also essential to know that a child's hearing is OK, particularly if you spot a child having difficulties with the work on rhyme and sound patterns. Working with sounds is an opportunity to promote good listening skills. Sounds can be represented as music beats and they can also be linked to number work and language development. Bang a drum. How many beats? Try alternating soft and loud beats. Is this a hard (*t* or *s*) or a soft (*m* or *n*) sound? Is the sound long or short? This focus on sounds is an essential start to the process of spelling, which follows later.

Always pronounce sounds in their 'pure' form rather than 'buh, duh, muh' etc. There is no 'uh' sound attached to the single consonant.

How to start

- Remember that until letters are introduced, sound work is oral.
- Model the clear pronunciation of words with the first and final sounds distinct.
- Show a picture of each word or the actual object to ensure meaning.
- Stick to single-letter clearly identified phonemes at first until the concept of the first sound within a word is understood (*m*oney, *p*enguin).
- Introduce more difficult phonemes which are represented by consonant digraphs (*ch*in, *ch*atter, *sh*op, *th*inking), and later on, other clusters (*cl*ap, *br*ick, *st*icker).
- Emphasise the first phoneme as you say the word. Then ask children to repeat the word. As they speak, listen for any pronunciation difficulties. This is a valuable opportunity for adults to notice speech difficulties that may need to be addressed.

General activities and resources for working with initial sounds could include:

- Games from *Phonic Progression* (see Resources) at Step 2.
- 'Show me' types of activities using pictures from calendars, magazines or even Christmas cards – children hold up their picture when you say the sound that their picture starts with.
- Real objects to enhance the interest, for example, toys or items you or they have brought into school.

Also use the activities to fill in any observed gaps in children's vocabulary.

Writing the letters that represent each sound

This skill masks two sub-skills:

- Knowing what each letter looks like and reproducing its likeness.
- Forming each letter with the correct sequence of hand movements.

Most children manage the former long before the latter. But once allowed to grow, the 'wrong' handwriting habits can do much damage. Handwriting features in the final section of this chapter.

The individual letters *a–z* are single phonemes as they each constitute a single sound. The letter digraphs *ch*, *sh* and *th* are still regarded as single phonemes as they also constitute a single sound. In my experience, these digraphs are notoriously difficult for some children to grasp and time spent on these will pay dividends later.

Never say to children that the sounds *c* and *h* make the sound *ch* (as in *chip*) because this is not correct. It is the two *letters* when combined into one grapheme that form the sound. So we might say that the two letters together make the sound or phoneme *ch* (or *sh* or *th*), and that when we hear the phoneme *ch* in a word we write it as the two letters *ch*. Always ensure that children have understood the concept of letter sounds properly before starting work on letter recognition and writing letters. All three should be tackled together. The child needs to:

- Hear the letter sound.
- See the letter shape that matches the sound.

- Feel the letter (using wooden or raised letters) as the sound is repeated.
- Write the letter using the correct sequence of movements.

Each part of the activity contributes towards a multisensory approach and leads to a thorough understanding of letters that will enable children to start to spell.

For some children, letter learning is a confusing experience. Too many letters look similar or identical apart from their orientation or rotation (*b*, *d* and *p*) for letter learning to be easy. Children must understand that a letter is that same letter only if it is constantly that way up all of the time and the point is worth stressing. More suggestions for developing letter knowledge are included within the handwriting section on letter formation later in this chapter.

Colour is always a useful way of showing children the difference between vowels and consonants, although we may not be focusing on these differences at this stage.

Identifying initial and dominant phonemes in spoken words

Consonants are the sounds we are most likely to identify first in spoken words. This is why, until children have fully reached the phonetic stage of spelling, consonants are the main letters represented. Which sounds in the following words do you think are the most dominant? Try saying each word aloud as you put yourself in the position of a Reception child. For each word, which letter sounds jump out at you the most?

hat / carpet / selfish / flower / table / clock / coffee / elephant / snow / microwave / computer

Although much depends on how we say each word, generally speaking the consonants are the dominant sounds.

Once children can write the letters, say some common words (clearly and slowly) and ask them to listen for the dominant sounds and write down the letters that match them. Activities such as these encourage children to have a go at spelling all kinds of words just by hearing dominant sounds. This is the starting point of phonetic approaches to spelling. Without the ability to hear and to identify dominant sounds within words, spelling will not develop.

Remember that for this particular objective, we want learners to identify *any* sounds, wherever they are within the word, not just the initial ones. Talking about which sounds have been picked out will enhance the benefit of the activities.

Identifying and writing initial and final phonemes in CVC words

Which words are CVC (consonant-vowel-consonant) words and which are not? CVC words are those with a short medial vowel sound between two consonant phonemes. Many CVC words have three single-letter phonemes as listed in the box below. For spelling purposes, single-syllable words with *sh*, *ch* and *th* (*ship*, *path*, *chop*) are also CVC words (also listed below). While these words have four letters, they only have three phonemes, as the *sh*, *ch* and *th* are single sounds.

Which three-letter words are not, in this context, CVC words? Given that a CVC word is one with a short medial vowel sound in the middle, words such as *for*, *car*, *her* do not belong in the CVC category for spelling purposes. The vowel sound *a* in *car* is changed by the sound *r* and is not the same as in the middle of *cat*, *sat*, *cap*, *rat*, *pan*.

Examples of CVC words with three letters

With medial vowel *a*	bat, cab, dam, fat, gap, hat, map, pan, rat, wax
With medial vowel *e*	bet, fed, get, keg, met, pen, pet, ten, red, wet
With medial vowel *i*	bin, dim, fig, fit, kit, nib, pit, sip, tin, win, zip
With medial vowel *o*	box, cot, dot, fog, got, hot, hop, not, rob, rod
With medial vowel *u*	bun, cut, dug, fun, gun, hub, nut, pud, run, yum

(NB: It is worth stating to children that no words begin with the letter x.)

Examples of CVC words with four letters

With *sh*	ship, shot, push, hash, bush, mash
With *ch*	chin, chum, chop, much, such, chip
With *th*	thin, this, path, bath, thug, them, this

When teaching CVC words, say each word clearly. When separating the sounds to identify each phoneme remember to pronounce the consonants as 'pure' sounds (not 'buh' or 'muh'). As far as possible, letters such as *c* in *cut* should be pronounced without the voice, just using air through the mouth. Stress all three phonemes equally. The final sound in CVC words is often not identified by learners because it is not stressed as clearly through normal speech. Pictures or objects will help to assign meaning to CVC activities.

Activities could include:

- Saying CVC words for children to write on white boards or on paper.
- Snap games – matching the same initial sound, the same end sound or both. Vary the rules with the same set of cards.
- Domino games with similar rules (see below).
- Place pictures of CVC words in a pile on the table. Hold up the beginning and end letters for each one. Children search for the matching pictures.
- Give each child five or six letters – children listen to CVC words and hold up the correct letter or letters (at the beginning, end or both).

Playing dominoes with CVC words

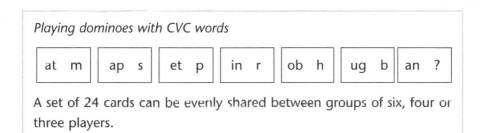

A set of 24 cards can be evenly shared between groups of six, four or three players.

Try not to let difficulties with letter formation interfere with activities that are focused on sounds. Children who are still struggling to write their letters could be given wooden or plastic letters to find rather than *always* having to write them. In this way, all children can experience success in identifying the sounds and being able to recognise the letters in CVC words, even if they are struggling to form some of them.

All work on letters must be part of a multisensory approach, for example, 'Jolly Phonics' (see Resources) is a kit that requires children to sing a rhyme, look at the letter (upper and lower case) and write the letter. The resource introduces children to both the lower and upper case versions of letters from the beginning.

While professionals have not always agreed on the efficacy of introducing lower and upper case letters at the same time, I personally believe that with sensitive and very clear teaching, confusions are no more likely than if lower and upper case letters are taught separately. There is a strong argument for teaching both lower and upper case letters, each with their sound, shape and name, all together, so that children can appreciate all of the attributes that contribute to each letter's *totality of meaning*. Meaning is the key factor!

The resources used to teach CVC knowledge are crucial to success. There is no substitute for adult intervention with sensitive talk sessions during which children can ask questions and eradicate potential confusions. It is all too easy for adults to explain a concept and to think that children have understood the main points when in reality they have not – complete understanding of CVC words is essential to further progression in phonic knowledge.

In this context, worksheets do very little to support children's understanding of CVC words, nor are they interactive and multisensory. Simply colouring in a picture or looking at it and writing its initial or end letter is of minimal value. There are many interactive and interesting resources that help to develop CVC knowledge (see Resources). If used at all, worksheets need to be selected with care to ensure that the right skills are being developed.

■ Alphabetic and phonic knowledge

There are two objectives for this:

- To sound and name letters of the alphabet in lower case.
- To understand alphabetical order.

Although we teach children to know the sounds, shapes and names of each letter at more or less the same time, many children have great difficulty with letter names. This is hardly surprising: from a child's viewpoint, only people and animals have names, so the purpose of a letter name can be a strange concept. When teaching letter names, you might say something like 'All letters have a sound and a shape. Letters also have a name. Just like you have a name.'

If you are teaching lower case and upper case letters together, you might hold up the letter to be focused on (both forms), and explain that this letter has one sound *a*, but it has two shapes – **a** and **A**. You might emphasise that the letter shapes make the same sound in words and that they share the same name. Many children may not realise this.

Some children will struggle to understand why a letter has a name. You could explain that its name is needed for spelling out words and for using a dictionary later. Without a name we wouldn't know what to call it and we wouldn't be able to find it. I often think that children need to know the purpose in order to grasp the concept.

Once letter names have been introduced, we need to discourage children from spelling out words using the letter sounds. The more we model how to use letter names the more children will eventually catch on to them. To help children get to grips with letter names we could:

- Dictate words to spell using letter names.
- Practise matching name to shape – say the names of letters for children to find the correct ones from a selection.
- Always spell out the high-frequency (tricky) words using the letter names, once these have been introduced, as this will help to discourage children from sounding out these types of words.

The second part of the objective is for children to understand alphabetical order. But do they always understand what the alphabet is? Why do we have an alphabet and how do we use it? Singing the alphabet is a useful and enjoyable activity, but if at the end of the exercise, that is all some children can do what has been the point? We could help children to understand the alphabet by:

- Linking it with letter names.
- Explaining its purpose and showing some examples of dictionaries. Even if children are not yet at the dictionary stage, they will still appreciate why the alphabet and the dictionary are linked meaningfully together.

- Practising activities to develop alphabetical order – start slowly to see if all children have got the idea. For example, some children may be able to work only with the first five letters (a–e) before eventually being able to place all letters into alphabetical order. For some children, having to place all 26 letters in sequence may take considerable practice and some may need an alphabet line to refer to at first.

- For children who struggle with letter formation, the task need not always be to write the letters on paper. They could sequence plastic or wooden letters instead to allow them to focus on the skill of sequencing rather than the arduous (for them) task of letter formation.

- Use pictures and objects as well for children to identify the first letter and place into alphabetical order.

Once children can place letters into alphabetical order this skill can be linked with the words children are currently learning in Reception, for example, the high-frequency or CVC words. The objective here would be to place words in the order in which they would appear in a dictionary as a first, simple step towards using a wordbook for finding spellings (see box below).

High-frequency words in a wordbook

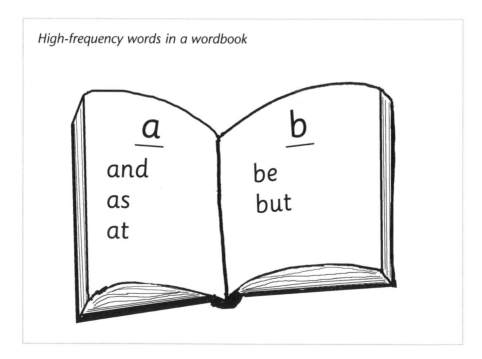

■ **Linking sound and spelling patterns**

We can help children to do this by:

- Using rhyme to identify families of CVC words.
- Teaching the onset and rime principle.
- Teaching alliteration.

Children need to grasp the idea that different sounds in words represent different spelling patterns. While this may seem obvious to us, it may not be to all children. Simply matching letter sounds to their shapes does not necessarily equate with linking sounds to spelling patterns. Many children simply do not make this transfer without support.

As an example, ask some children who have been taught their letters through the 'Jolly Phonics' scheme to say the sound of a given letter. Some cannot say the letter sound *without the activity* that went with the teaching of it. For the letter *t* they will move their heads from side to side as if they are watching *t*ennis, as that was the action that accompanied the teaching sessions. I have known some children continue to do this well into Year 1.

Rhyming CVC words

Hopefully, the following activities will help children to link sounds with spelling patterns. We might start with rhyming CVC words, emphasising to learners that CVC words that rhyme must have the same medial vowel sounds as well as the last letters:

CVC rhyming families

at	it	am	in	ot	ug
cat	bit	dam	din	pot	jug
bat	kit	ham	sin	rot	hug
sat	sit	Sam	pin	cot	tug
mat	pit	ram	bin	hot	bug
hat	fit	jam	fin	got	rug

Strategies could include:

● Sorting CVC word cards into rhyming families as shown above.

● Playing games with the word cards, for example, snap or pairs.

● Picking the odd one out.

● Colouring or highlighting the rhyming parts of CVC words.

Gradually include the full range of CVC, including words with *sh*, *th* and *ch*. There is no reason why we can't reinforce upper case letters as part of these activities.

This exercise of rounding up rhyming CVC families has reminded me of the many exceptions, some of which children will bring to the activities. It's no wonder that learners get confused and easy to see why spelling eventually must evolve towards a visual strategy:

– *jam, ham* but *wham, lamb*

– *met, get* but *debt*

– *rum, tum* but *thumb*

– *path, bath* but *wrath*

– *zip, hip* but *whip*

You might welcome such exceptions from children, but explain that as the spellings are different they do not fit the CVC category.

Distinguishing onsets from rimes in speech and spelling

This may be a difficult concept for children to grasp: the 'onset' is the first phoneme, but not necessarily the first letter only; the 'rime' is the rest of the word. Some examples of words split into onsets and rimes are shown below:

Distinguishing onsets from rimes	
Same onset, but different rime	*chips, choose, cheese, chatter*
	thing, thug, thump
Same rime but, different onset	*fan, man, tan, pan*
	sheet, meet, feet

Of course, at three-letter CVC level, words that rhyme are also bound to be onset and rime words as there are no vowel choices. But let's think about how the idea of onset and rime supports spelling. First by analogy – if we can spell *beach*, then we can spell *teach* and *peach*. Similarly, if we can spell *me*, then *be*, *she* and *he* follow the same pattern. Onset and rime activities help to strengthen children's awareness of word patterns.

Children could:

- Reassemble 'jigsaw' words as illustrated below.
- Play snap with different rules, for example, to say 'snap' when two words with the same onset (or the same rime) are turned over together.
- Collect families of the same onset or the same rime.

Remember that the notion of onset and rime is concerned with spelling patterns as well as speech. Rhyme is to do with speech only.

Jigsaw onset and rime

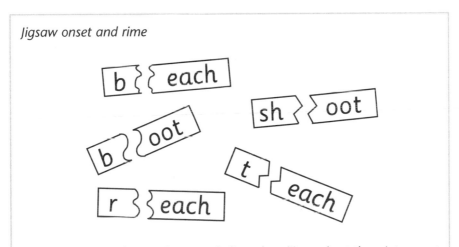

(Quick tip: Write the words on cards first, then 'jigsaw' cut them into onset and rime.)

Alliteration

What is alliteration, you may ask? These are sentences that are made up of words beginning with the same letter, for example, *Cool cats can catch cabbages* or *Peter Piper picked a peck of pickled pepper*. Alliteration reinforces initial letter awareness. Activities might include:

- Underlining the alliterative letters in phrases and sentences.

- Inventing silly alliterative sentences such as those above.

- Oral round-up – each child in a group adds a word which follows the alliterative pattern, for example, *we went walking...*

- Children attaching funny alliterative adjectives to their names – *Brilliant Brenda, Demon Dave, Raving Royston.*

Hopefully, after having engaged in a range of enjoyable activities such as those suggested, most children will have grasped the idea that different sounds have different spelling patterns as a starting point to eventually being able to match the full range. This is what we want them to learn as a start to their phonetic approach to spelling.

On the other hand we also want them to learn that some words (in fact, a huge proportion) do not follow regular phonic patterns and are not spelled as they sound. It's little wonder that children become confused.

Recognising critical features of words by shape, length and common spelling patterns

For this we need to focus on visual approaches to spelling. Throughout Reception, so much effort is devoted to developing phonological awareness and phonic knowledge that the visual skills necessary for acquiring the tricky words are neglected. Many children continually try to sound out words such as *said* or *they*. So what can we do? Draw an eye, preferably on a large and colourful sheet of paper! Yes, I really mean it.

Emphasise to children that they must never try to sound out these tricky words. Whenever you are working on these words, get out the 'eye' and display it as a reminder. You could also explain why these words are tricky. Many of us are familiar with 'sed' and 'cum' as the results of a misplaced strategy for sounding out words. So, going for the visual approach, what do we want children to *look at*? Study the list of words from the first NLS list (intended to be acquired by the end of the Reception year) shown below and consider why some of these words are difficult to learn to spell (and to read).

High-frequency words to learn throughout the Reception year

I / up / look / we / like / and / am / at / for / he / is / said / go / you / are / this / going / they / away / play / a / am / cat / to / come / day / the / dog / big / my / mum / no / dad / all / get / in / went / was / of / me / she / see / it / yes / can

---

Strategies for teaching these words could include:

- Placing them in families building on the idea of onset and rime, for example, *me, she, he*.
- Drawing attention to the tricky parts of each word. Spell the word using plastic or wooden letters and ask children to study it, then remove the tricky bit, for example, the *ai* in *said*, and see if they can say which letters are missing.
- Matching words to 'empty' shapes, as illustrated below.
- Playing some of the games already suggested, for example, dominoes or snap.
- Looking for some of these little words that are 'hidden' inside longer words (see below).
- Using word search activities – excellent for developing visual skills.

Empty shapes for tricky words

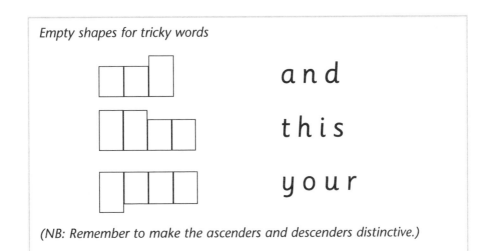

(NB: Remember to make the ascenders and descenders distinctive.)

Little words inside longer words		
the	in	they, their, there, them, then
he	in	her, here
you	in	your, yours
at	in	cat, pat
all	in	ball, call, stall
and	in	candle, sand, hand, panda
we	in	were, went

(Chant and sing There's a 'he' in her, there's an 'all' in ball and so on.)

The objective is for children to be able to spell the high-frequency words listed above quickly as an aid to independent writing. So this is a good time to teach children how to learn particular words using the LSCWC strategy. Teach children to:

- Look at the word.
- Say it aloud a few times as they study its critical features (they might also spell out the word using the letter names).
- Cover it.
- Write the word from memory.
- Check that it's correct and rewrite it if not.

At this point I usually talk about 'putting the words inside their heads' and 'keeping them there'.

If these visual skills are focused upon, the majority of learners will gradually learn to spell these words with their eyes closed as the critical features of each one is assigned to memory. At this point in our exploration, I am reminded of the already stated principle 'use it or lose it'. If we want children to learn these tricky words, they must be required to spell them regularly within their writing.

The word level objectives for the Reception year also focus on vocabulary. The collections of new words that children add to their vocabulary offer opportunities for children to categorise and to study words with regard to the skills referred to in this chapter. Some children may notice that a longer word has a CVC beginning, for example, *com*puter or *his*tory (especially if you draw their attention to such features).

Reinforcing spelling within the context of 'subject' words is always a positive move. It's good for children to think of spelling as a skill needed in every area of learning and not just as a subject within itself. I often wonder what children think about when they are spelling. Why did Jasmine spell the word 'like' correctly during a spelling test then on the same day as 'lac' within a sentence? We cannot see into children's minds but we can help young learners to perceive spelling as a cross-curricular area of thinking, not simply as the time spent in the literacy hour, the 20 minutes of ALS time or some other focused practice session.

Handwriting in the Reception year

At the beginning of this chapter we started with the objectives for letter learning. It is worth repeating that all work on letters must be interactive and multisensory, and that the skills of learning to recognise and to write letters must be complementary to each other. Three basic skills help to form good handwriting for life:

- A comfortable and efficient pencil grip.
- The production of controlled lines which support letter formation.
- The formation of letters with the correct sequence of movements.

Handwriting practice can be boring, especially for those children who find it difficult and have to practise over and over again. Liven up the process where possible by using coloured paper, different pencils, crayons, or markers and white boards. When working on handwriting with whatever scheme:

- Link handwriting with the letters and words already learned rather than using words with which the children are not familiar.
- Address letter formation problems immediately they are noticed.
- When writing letters, ensure that children start and finish letters in the correct position. If they don't and letters persist in being formed the wrong way round, developing these into joined script at a later stage will be all the more difficult.

- Talk about the formation and chant the process together as children focus on each letter (see box below).

- Talk about **ascenders** and **descenders** as 'sticks' or 'tails' or whatever terminology will help children to remember them.

- Ensure that children have the correct pencil grip. Look at the pressure as they write and the flexible movement of the thumb and forefinger.

- Talk about the similarities and differences between various letters to help children to remember the minute details.

- During other activities, draw children's attention to letters they may be having trouble with, for example, when reading their book, especially if they need to focus on a particular letter to read a difficult word.

Chanting the direction of letter movements

b	**down**, up, round
d	round, **up**, down
g	round, up, **down**, give it a tail
p	**down**, up, round

(Stress the key part of the letter movement that characterises the formation of the letter.)

Assigning an image to a letter shape is also helpful for some children. Focus on this image as they write the letter. For example: *l* looks like a lamp post, *s* looks like a snake, *b* is written with the bat before the ball, *a* looks like an apple with its stem, *o* looks like an orange and *u* looks like a cup. One child once commented that the letters *a* and *g* (handwritten versions) have 'big, fat tummies'. If imagery helps children to remember, then anything goes.

Finally, children need the process to be as multisensory as possible by:

- Feeling the letter in different materials – sand, furry letters, on children's backs.

- Saying the name of each letter as it is being written.

- Saying the sound of each letter.

- Seeing examples of each letter in slightly different fonts all around the classroom.
- Talking about the similarities of and differences between various letters to help children to notice and remember the minute details of each one.
- Having their attention drawn to particular letters within words, especially the notoriously difficult ones such as *b* and *d* and so on.

In practice, activities need to be selected that will develop each set of objectives alongside the principles explored in the previous chapter. Obviously there will be a considerable overlap, but we need to understand each set of skills separately in order to assess children's spelling development and move learners on to the next phase. This does not, however, imply that these skills should be taught separately.

Summary

In this chapter I have looked at:

- The objectives for spelling and handwriting throughout the Reception year.
- Early handwriting skills and the formation of letters.

Chapter 5

Developing spelling in Years 1 and 2

This chapter considers:

- The main NLS objectives for spelling in Years 1 and 2 which guide learners through the semi-phonetic and phonetic phases towards transitional spelling.
- Strategies for developing these skills.

It is vitally important that as many children as possible have acquired the spelling skills and knowledge from Reception by the time they enter Year 1. The box below shows selected examples from the Year 1 objectives.

NLS spelling objectives for Year 1

Year 1, Term 1	Segment all three phonemes in CVC words (h-a-t) in order to spell them.
	Recognise critical features of words, for example, shape, length and common spelling patterns, as well as words within words (*in* within sink, *the* in there).
	Spell common irregular words from Appendix List 1.
Year 1, Term 2	Spell words with initial consonant clusters (e.g. blot, crab).
	Spell words with final consonant clusters (e.g. milk, hand).
	Spell words with *s* for plurals.
Year 1, Term 3	Common spelling patterns, long vowel phonemes – ee, ai, ie, oa, oo (as in moon).
	Spelling of verbs with past tense *ed* and present tense *ing*.

Before we consider how to move children's spelling forward, what do we do about those children who have not acquired all the prerequisite foundation skills?

Gaps in letter knowledge are particularly common at this early stage. Some children may need catch-up time to secure their knowledge of letter sounds and their formation of letters; this could take place alongside Year 1 work. Assuming that some catch-up strategies are in place, and having considered the objectives listed above for spelling work in Year 1, the following sections outline suggestions for supporting each term's work.

Year 1, Term 1

Throughout Year 1, Term 1, the focus is on segmenting CVC words for spelling. Remember that a CVC word is one with a short medial vowel sound in the middle. To segment these words, children have to hear the phonemes separately within words and identify which phonemes are at the beginning, middle and end of a word. Work on rhyming sets can be continued as this reinforces the onset and rime principle mentioned in the previous chapter.

The objective above emphasises all three CVC phonemes, not just the first and last one. Identifying the medial vowel is a common difficulty for many children. The way in which adults with different accents pronounce their medial vowels can exacerbate the problem, so pictures or objects will be helpful if you pronounce your vowel sounds differently from the learners. Placing CVC words within a sentence also helps those children with limited vocabularies to cue into the meaning of the focused words.

Strategies might include some of the games and activities already mentioned in the previous chapter (snap, pairs, happy families, jigsaw word cards and so on). Such activities support both blending (for reading) and segmentation (for spelling). See examples below.

Playing pairs with CVC words

cat   hop   ship   jam

   sip   map   mash

     hat   ham   pop

First identify the rule for the game (i.e. whatever you need to focus on). Does each pair need to have the:

    Same medial vowel?
    Same first letters?
    Same last letters?
    Same rimes?
    Same onsets?

How could you pair up the words above?

Playing happy families with CVC words

What is a family? Again, does each 'family' have words with the same vowel, first letter, onset or rime? Remember to state how many cards are required to make up a complete family. Four? Six? For this game, the word cards are shared out equally between players; children take turns to collect the cards needed to make up their chosen family. Players either choose to pick up the next card on the pile and 'throw away' a card in their hand that is not part of the family being collected, or 'pass' and keep the cards they have in their hand. On what basis do the words for each column constitute 'happy families' of four?

mash	cop	mash
dash	hot	push
bash	posh	dish
cash	dot	shop

One column has words with the same rime (left); one has words with the same digraph at the beginning or end of the word (right); one column has words with the same vowel (middle). Children can use the same set of cards for different rules. What matters is that children know why they are placing words together to make up a family and can identify their family's common factor (they can think of it as the family surname, e.g. the *sh* family).

Matching CVC phonemes

When splitting words for jigsaw activities, think about how you are going to split the phonemes. Do you need to focus on the onset and rime principle to split each of the three sounds or to reinforce a particular sound/letter pattern? The teaching point should indicate how the words are 'jigsawed'. So, if the task is to separate the *sh*, *ch*, *th* so that learners see these as single phonemes in four-letter CVC words, which example is the odd one out from the following set?

sh   op   th   in   sh   ip   p   ush   sh   in   ch   op   th   at

You have probably noticed that 'p ush' separates a single letter onset from the rime rather than the consonant digraph from the rest of the word as the others in the family do. How many different CVC words can you make using the letters above?

Revisiting favourite and familiar games and activities, albeit in a new context, can offer less confident learners security through being allowed to remain within their known comfort zone. Other strategies for CVC work with the focus on segmentation might include:

- Dictating short sentences containing CVC words which also practise the tricky words – *The sun is hot. Has a fish got legs? The cat can run.* Make them funny and have a good laugh as the children spell.
- Ask children to write their own game cards to play 'true' or 'false'. They write a short sentence containing only tricky and CVC words on strips of card, thus practising their spelling for a real purpose. Each player then reads a sentence and says if it is true or false. If correct, the player 'wins' the card. Who wins most cards wins the game.

● Remember to include the CVC words with *sh* and *ch* in this context – at the end as well as at the beginning.

A key principle for children to grasp at this stage is that consonants, either single or as clusters and digraphs, must have a vowel between them. It is worth making sure that learners understand this basic principle as it supports more advanced spelling. Use colour to indicate the difference between vowels and consonants. If some children do have problems with the medial vowels in CVC words, try focusing on one medial vowel at a time to reduce the potential for confusion.

Year 1, Term 2

This term introduces words with double consonants at the end (*ff, ss, ll*), as well as simple words with *ck* as in *sick* (still three phonemes), and words with *ng* as in *long* (four phonemes). We could encourage learners to think of *ck* words as CVC words in the sense that they have only three phonemes but four letters. A useful principle is that words with the final phoneme *k* are likely to be spelt as *ck* most of the time when the vowel is a short one – *pick, sock, lock, back*. Similar activities to those already suggested can be reworked.

The introduction of words with *ng* is the first group of double end clusters. These may be difficult for some learners as the *n* is a soft sound. Many children tend to spell *sing* as *sig* or *hang* as *hag* because the letter *g* is the more dominant of the pair. We need to make an important point about the letter *q*. As this letter is rarely, if ever, found without its partner *u*, I always present the two together (at whatever spelling level) so that children get used to *qu* as one grapheme.

Finally, Year 1, Term 2 introduces the double consonant clusters at the beginning of words, for example, *bl*ock, *cr*ab, *fr*og, *sh*ip and *pr*am. The introduction of double consonants heralds a distinctly different level as children are now working with words that have more than one phoneme and grapheme at the beginning.

The principle of beginning, middle and end (illustrated below) is crucial at this point as children need to identify and segment the two phonemes at the beginning of each word. Four-letter words with double consonant clusters at the beginning are sometimes referred to as CCVC words as they consist of consonant-consonant-vowel-consonant.

Consonant clusters at the beginning of words: examples of CCVC words		
blot, blip, bled	brim, brat, brag	clip, clap, club
crab, crib, crag	drop, drab, drip	flog, flit, flat
frog, from, fret	glum, glen, glad	grip, grin, grub
plan, plum, plug	pram, prod, prim	scan, scab, scam
skip, skin, skid	slim, slap, slab	smug, smut, smog
snap, snip, snot	spot, spin, spud	stop, step, stab
swim, swam, swum	trim, trip, tram	twin, twig, twit

As you can see, many words fall within the CCVC category, but equally there are many exceptions that children will point out in spelling sessions that will need to be explained. The word *swan* fits the CCVC category but is not pronounced as it is spelled. When using the term CCVC we need to be clear what we mean. It's helpful if children recognise exceptions as it reminds them that not all words follow regular phonic patterns. Similarly, many single-syllable words with double consonant clusters are not CCVC words – *dwell, dwarf, skull* – as they have more than four letters.

Once children have understood the CCVC groups of words, longer words with double consonant clusters can be included as random samples to help to reinforce the idea of double consonant clusters at the beginning – *bright, brown, brain*. Jigsaw word cards are a good activity for practising these spellings with the consonant cluster separated from the rest of the word. Remember that learning to spell these types of words depends on children recognising the first two (or three as in *string*) phonemes as a double (or triple) beginning to the word.

Support strategies could include:

- Starting with one 'family' of words and adding to them as children begin to get the idea. For example, you might start with the *bl* family then progress through the families starting with *br, cl, cr* and so on.
- Having considered a few families of words, relate these to the onset and rime principle (same rime) – *brick, stick, slick, trick, flick*.
- Remind children that the vowel sounds are still short (they sound the same as for the CVC words they have already learned).

- Limit examples to CCVC patterns until children have grasped the main idea – *brim, stop, pram, frog.*
- Once children are comfortable with double consonant clusters include longer words with the same onsets – *brick, branch, bracket.*

When providing feedback to children from their practice sessions, always focus first and foremost on the spelling pattern that forms the objective of the teaching session. For example, when you reach the stage of including longer words as part of the work on consonant clusters, do not bother about the totally correct spellings – focus on the consonant clusters at the beginning of each word.

The point of including more random examples is to develop children's phonological awareness and continue to encourage their have-a-go approaches to spelling. The general skills of hearing all phonemes within words should still be developing alongside the specific phonic knowledge that is taught systematically.

Children are also taught how to spell words with the consonant clusters at the ends of the words as shown below, sometimes referred to as CVCC words (consonant-vowel-consonant-consonant).

Consonant clusters at the end of words: examples of CVCC words	
best, cast, list, must, mist	hunt, sent, mint, went
camp, wimp, lamp, bump	sing, bang, long, ring
milk, sulk, hulk, silk	film, helm
disk, mask, husk	bank, sink, pink
held, mild, bald, cold, sold	felt, belt, melt, silt
hand, send, rind, wind, find	Wilf, wolf, golf

Not all the CVCC categories are represented and you will notice that some words do not fit the sets. Which words are the odd ones out as CVCC words with short medial vowel sounds? You probably identified *mild, bald, cold, sold* and *wolf,* as well as *rind* and *find.*

For some children, sounds at the end of words are more difficult to recognise than those at the beginning. Similar principles apply to the teaching of these word patterns, and the same types of activities can be reworked. *Phonic Progression* (see Resources) contains many more games to develop spelling at CCVC and CVCC levels. Once these ideas are grasped, start to combine the double consonant clusters at the beginning and the end of words – *blast, cramp, bring, stink* – and also show children how these patterns form parts of longer words – *crumpet, helmet.* Remember to reinforce previous knowledge continually, for example, *sh, ch* and *th* – *filth, shelf.*

At this point, I'd like to mention the issue of slang. Children in my class have often brought words such as *snot* or *spud* to discussion sessions and providing they are not tasteless, offensive or rude, I see no harm in using words that are part of the general slang of the English language. After all, some children do talk about peeling the *spuds.*

The final focus during Year 1, Term 2 is on *ed* and *ing* word endings. The *ing* ending does not seem to cause as many difficulties as the *ed* ending perhaps because children have already come across *ring, sing, thing* etc. What they now need to realise is that the same spelling pattern (*ing*) is used at the end of words in a totally different context, i.e. to denote the continuous present tense (danc*ing*, sing*ing*, hold*ing*).

The *ed* ending is often more difficult for some learners to grasp because the graphemes (letters) do not sound exactly like the phonemes. Consider how the following *ed* words are pronounced – *stopped, sailed, carried.* See the box below for a range of words with *ed* endings.

Words with 'ed' endings

How many different speech and spelling patterns can you spot and which spellings require the root part of the word to change?

pushed / mashed / talked / walked / mixed / missed / grasped / gulped / spotted / heated / carried / married / hoped / hopped / stopped / shipped / stepped

---

The range is far from complete, but we can see why children confuse the *ed* endings. Some root words lose a letter, *hope* → *hoped*, while some root words gain a letter, *stop* → *stopped.*

When teaching these groups of spellings:

- Explain to children that spelling words with *ed* endings is not a sounding-out strategy (this is often why we get *t* and *id* at the end of words). Meaning is the key factor. Children must understand where the *ed* ending fits into a sentence and to think of this not simply as a cluster of letters but as part of the verb structure when they are writing in the past tense. This is a clear example of why some work on spelling needs to be linked to text level writing.

- Start with the more simple *ed* endings which do not involve changes to the root part of the word – *bumped, dressed.*

- If some vowel digraphs have been covered, these families could be included – *sailed, spoiled, clouded, weeded.*

- When working on those *ed* endings which involve changing the root part of the word (e.g. doubling the end consonant as in *pat/patted, stop/stopped*), show families of the same pattern so that children can begin to understand these spelling rules as they progress. But remember that for those learners who find it difficult, the main spelling objective at this point is the *ed* ending, not the doubling of the consonant.

- At first, try to avoid families of words that have other spelling rules. For example, the 'y changing to ie' rule (*carry/carried, hurry/hurried*) may confuse some children until the simpler versions of the *ed* ending have been understood.

Both the *ing* and the *ed* endings need to be learned visually and with attention to meaning as part of present and past tense verb structures. The reason why many children fail to grasp these spellings could be that because they do not understand their grammatical role they do not know when to apply them during the writing process.

At this stage of spelling children really do need to think. When teaching the specific patterns of words referred to above (CVCC and CCVC), continue to reinforce the BME principle (e.g. *br-a-g, ch-u-nk*). This principle becomes more complex as children start to add endings onto the basic forms of words. You might ask: how does this apply to *ed* and *ing* endings? In this case, children could be taught to think of the BME for the root of the word, and apply the ending (*cr-a-ck-ing*). This, of course, transports children's levels of thinking to that of syllables, which is one of the word level objectives for spelling in Year 2.

▓ Year 1, Term 3

Finally in Year 1, children are introduced to the range of **vowel digraphs**, many of which are also referred to as long vowel phonemes. This is because the combined vowels often have a longer sound than the short medial vowels in CVC words (see examples below).

Examples of vowel digraph families

ee – peel, cheep, free, feet

oi – boil, spoil, coin, hoist

ai – pail, stain, paint, brain

ow – clown, drown, grown

ue – blue, clue, glue

oa – soap, coat, gloat, poach

oo – pool, fool, spoon, roost

ea – team, peach, steal, cream

ou – cloud, mound, ground

ew – dew, drew, grew

aw – crawl, saw, drawn, trawl

At this point, phonemes and graphemes are becoming quite complex and there are many opportunities to introduce previous knowledge. Once the single-syllable words in these categories are understood, try some random, longer words – *flower*, *teacher*, *cloudy*, and try to reinforce any word endings already taught – *flowering*.

The sets of words above are notoriously difficult for some children because they introduce additional facts concerning the vowels that have been taught in the CCVC and CVCC contexts. The knowledge that the medial letter *a* has a different sound when partnered with the letter *i* (as in *rain, mail, brain*) can be confusing. I use the word 'partner' when teaching these in order to show that the two vowels together form a completely different sound, as *one phoneme.*

For some children, this work will be starting to become very difficult so continue to make it as interesting as possible. Spelling does not always have to be a pencil and paper task! Keep that motivation going: use large sheets of paper as a group activity; write with coloured marker pens; spell in the air; work as pairs, rather than always as individuals to provide peer support for some children. Many of the activities already suggested can be used to develop children's knowledge of vowel digraphs. Jigsaw activities work particularly well as these reinforce the BME principle.

Vowel digraph jigsaw words

Remember the BME principle when splitting single-syllable vowel digraph words.

cl oa k	sl ee p	st ai n	tr ea t
br ea d	sp oi l	cr ow n	gr ou nd

The key point is not to separate the vowel digraph 'partners' – children need to see both letters 'holding hands together'.

When helping children to spell single-syllable words with vowel digraphs, I point out that the main vowel partners are usually found in the middle of the word and that any consonant clusters or digraphs are at the beginning or the end:

r *ai* n   st *ea* l   cr *ow* d   pr *ou* d   sp *oi* l   p *ea* ch   sh *ee* p

Of course, this is not always the case – *blue, threw, boy* and *each, oil.*

At some point, as phonic knowledge becomes more complex, THRASS (Teaching Handwriting, Reading and Spelling Skills) can become a useful resource. THRASS is a support programme (see Resources) that can be introduced to children from the Foundation years. If using THRASS as a main spelling resource, it should form part of the spelling policy of the school, although we can dip into it. The resource focuses on:

- Knowledge of the alphabet sequence.
- Naming letters.
- Using the correct terms (e.g. phoneme, grapheme).
- Handwriting skills.
- Awareness of the 44 phonemes in the English language.
- Spelling choices for a range of phonemes.

It works on the principle that the 26 single letters of the alphabet can be combined to form 44 phonemes in the English language, and that by knowing all of these phonemes and matching them correctly to graphemes, children can learn to spell the vast majority of English words.

A brief mention of graphs (one letter), digraphs (two letters) and trigraphs (three letters) is useful here. Consider the word *knight*. The six letters make up only three phonemes – *kn-igh-t*. The word is made up of one digraph (*kn*), one trigraph (*igh*), and one graph (*t*). With regard to vowel digraphs, one phoneme can invite a choice of graphemes, and each of those graphemes can be graphs, digraphs or trigraphs. Believe me, all of this is very useful for learners who have to think about spelling choices. And by this vowel digraph stage, logical *thinking* is what it's all about.

Consider the five examples of how the phoneme *ee* can be represented as a grapheme – sh*ee*p, p*ea*ch, br*ie*f, b*e*, k*ey*. So we could spell *sheep* as *sh ey p*, *sh ie p*, *sh ea p* – any of the three would be a logical choice if we did not know how to spell it. THRASS works on the premise that spelling development relies on an understanding of the phoneme/grapheme principle (that one sound can have two or more letters) and can be used to teach this principle to those children who need to be taught the range of spelling choices explicitly.

A significant feature of THRASS is the visual approach to spelling. Once children start to battle with the complexities of different grapheme choices, the visual approach must start to take over from the phonetic one. As the visual approach begins to dominate, this initiates the essential progress from the phonetic to the transitional phase of spelling. Certainly by Years 3 to 4, the visual approach should be dominant in children's thinking, and many learners will be well into the transitional phase.

What should we do if children spell *peach* as *piech*, *leaf* as *leef* or *boil* as *boyl*? These errors are part of the learning process. If children start to use the range of vowel digraphs in their spelling, incorrectly or not, it shows that they have remembered these choices and taken them on board as part of their thinking. It demonstrates progress at this early stage of getting to grips with vowel digraphs. My strategy for moving children on would be to select a vowel digraph 'family' (from among the errors) and lead them towards the most likely choices using analogy and **investigations**. For example, there are fewer *ie* words, so the most likely choices are *ee* and *ea*.

Investigations at this point (of words with the *ee* phonemes and graphemes) would help children to see the letter patterns within words, hence the *likeliest* choices. Learning visually, each family of vowel digraph words that they have focused on as part of an investigation will help children to acquire more visually learned words; they are more able to make an informed guess when spelling new words. All children should continue to attempt new words without adult help.

Finally, remember that there are always the exceptions to contend with, for example, *broach/brooch*. But whoever thought that spelling was boring? Taught with zest and fervour, it's all fascinating stuff.

▉ Spelling in Year 2

The spelling objectives for Year 2 seek to:

● Extend phonic knowledge.

● Develop further the strategies for segmenting words into their phonemes.

● Continue the focus on the high-frequency tricky words listed in Appendix 1 in the NLS framework (the list for Years 1 and 2 is huge).

Year 2 children are also introduced to more of the unique peculiarities of English spelling. Consider the objectives listed below.

NLS spelling objectives for Year 2

Year 2, Term 1 Words with the same sound but different spellings (e.g. *hair* and *hare*).

Year 2, Term 2 Compound words – *postman, teaspoon, necklace*. Identifying syllables within words – *tiger, family*. Common prefixes (e.g. use of *un* and *dis* to indicate the negative).

Year 2, Term 3 Children investigate more spelling patterns (e.g. words with different sounds but the same spelling – *tear* and *tear*).

The emphasis is now far more focused on the patterns of spelling together with word meanings.

Many teachers and teaching assistants tell me that it is a difficult task to get through the whole NLS programme of objectives, even with those children who are quick to learn. Often there is not enough time to consolidate the previous teaching for those who either failed to understand the concepts in the first place or have not retained them. On the other hand, if children have not fully understood the phonic knowledge from Year 1, it will be extremely difficult for them to deal with compound words (necklace, teaspoon), and to understand prefix and suffix work.

From Year 2 the notion of chunking is particularly important as this strategy forms the basis for reading and spelling multi-syllabic words. **Chunking** involves visualising groups of letters within single-syllable words as one discrete unit. Those children who have grasped the phonic knowledge taught so far will start to see (on the page and in their minds) the following words as one chunk, each with a beginning, middle and end:

head / grasp / milk / peach / crash

They will also be able to add on the *ed* and *ing* endings without difficulty because they are able to chunk the main root words:

heading / headed / grasping / grasped / milking / milked / crashing / crashed

Learners who have mastered these basic principles will begin to understand (in English) how clusters of letters fit together in a sensible and logical way. Alongside learning to spell identified word families, this thinking process should be developing partly as common sense. How would you chunk the words below?

Using chunking strategies to spell multi-syllabic words			
replacement	adventure	semi-consciousness	
uncomfortable	incoherent	disappeared	instruction
unethical	achievable	assignation	signature

Did you identify the root of the word to allow you to separate the prefix or suffix? Or did you separate them out in a different order? Either way, you had to chunk the words to be able to identify the syllables and to read them. To spell them, you would have to 'see' in your mind the root words and the 'add-ons' as separate parts of the whole words in order to identify each phoneme, and then try to choose the right graphemes.

Some words at multi-syllabic level are easily understood and common to the language of most learners; others are more abstract in meaning and also act as nouns, verbs, adjectives or adverbs when in a sentence. Meaning is essential when working on the spelling of such words. Spelling is a highly complex process, but I hope that, like me, you are also beginning to see it as a fascinating, if elusive, element of the English language.

How might we develop the above objectives? Again, many of the games and activities already suggested can be recycled:

- *Same sound, but different spelling.* In order to deal with these sets of words, children need to understand the vocabulary as part of their spoken language. Focus on meaning as well as pattern. The only clue to which spelling is the correct one within the sentence being written (e.g. hair or hare), is its meaning. Try to show the rimes beneath each other in a column so that learners can see the pattern and always present these words within a sentence.

- *Compound words*, for example: backwards / forwards / carpet / fisher-man / gatehouse / earache / sunshine / lamplight / underneath / greenhouse / necklace. These words have to be chunked. Try matching word cards:

Matching up halves of compound words

How easily do you think children could match up these words?

in / lace / side / self / cake / hot / house / your / neck / pot / out / my / pan / green

Children need to understand that compound words are made up of two complete smaller words.

- *Syllables.* By this stage most children have realised that vowels appear between consonants and that a vowel, or vowel digraph, is present in each syllable (generally speaking). These two principles need to be re-inforced as teaching progresses. Teach children to 'hear' beats in spoken words. They could clap each beat – two in *circus, carpet* and *washing,* three in *family, computer* and *happiness.* How many beats in *investigation*? Work on syllables depends on the notion of beats being understood. Teach two-syllable words first until children have grasped the idea then move on to three-syllable words and so on.

- Similar suggestions apply to the work on *prefixes* and *suffixes.* These also depend on chunking skills for success. Understanding is also essential. What do 'un' and 'dis' actually mean? We might say that they mean nothing at all. A common function of prefixes and suffixes within words is to change the meaning of the root form, for example, *tangle* to *untangle, affect* to *disaffect, integrate* to *disintegrate.* Many prefixes shift meaning to the converse or opposite of the root word. Children will only use prefixes and suffixes correctly in their spelling if they are taught through meaning.

The NLS, rightly, places great emphasis on pace and progression, but individual progress in spelling relies on an understanding of the principles and strategies at each level. Without such understanding, children will come across barriers (in terms of knowledge gaps) that may be too much for some to cope with. As you work, remember also to integrate the new with the familiar. For example, when working with multi-syllabic words, identify those that have CVC beginnings (*hab*itat, *com*puter). Reinforce vowel digraph knowledge regularly to enable chunking skills to become speedy and efficient.

Investigations

Finally, as investigations feature significantly throughout spelling work at this level, and have been referred to in this chapter, let's look at how we might conduct these. Investigations involve learners in gathering examples of a chosen area of spelling and reflecting on these examples in order to draw conclusions, in this case, on logical spelling patterns and rules.

Investigating and exploring in groups should involve lots of focused talk about spelling and lead children on to asking questions and debating answers. Guiding questions and prompts from adults support the process.

Investigations could follow a sequence in which children:

- Find examples of the required spelling pattern (e.g. *ai* words or words with *ed* endings).

- Sort and categorise the examples, perhaps by colour highlighting.

- Search for the patterns and relationships that are significant (e.g. where in the words collected does each *ai* grapheme appear – beginning, middle or end?).

- Test the rule they have suggested – does it work for all words or are there exceptions?

- Assimilate the information as new spelling knowledge.

Children could investigate:

- Different families of vowel digraphs in order to develop more awareness of which groups of consonants and vowels are more likely to be compatible.

- Syllables – make lists of two-, three-, four-syllable words etc.

- Compound words – collect these from across the curriculum.

- Prefixes and suffixes – collect these in sets and talk about the meanings.

Investigations take time but the benefits are many, not least because children are given the opportunity to talk about spelling and to think about what they have found out. Spelling activities that focus primarily on children learning specific groups of words have limited value in terms of developing competent spellers. Spelling depends on thinking, and, for the majority of learners, thinking is stimulated by talk. Remind children that spelling is everywhere! Examples need to come from every subject. How many compound words can they find from history, geography, art etc? How many words with the vowel digraphs *ee* and *ea* can they collect from across the curriculum?

Summary

In this chapter I have looked at:

- The consolidation of skills and knowledge from Reception and throughout Years 1 and 2.
- The basic principles that must be fully understood before children move on to Key Stage 2.
- The basis of competent spelling development.

Chapter 6

Supporting spelling in Key Stage 2

This chapter charts NLS requirements for spelling throughout Key Stage 2 by:

- Summarising the NLS objectives for Years 3 to 6.
- Suggesting strategies for developing the key skills.

As you work through this chapter, note the major emphasis on rules and conventions based on the assumption that most children have already acquired the initial skills and knowledge, and will be ready to *think* and *reflect* more about spelling in terms of the patterns of English language and associated meanings.

By the time they enter Key Stage 2, many learners should be working well within the phonetic level of spelling and some will be spelling confidently at transitional level.

Spelling in Years 3 to 4

Children are expected to:

- Identify wrongly spelt words in their own writing using spelling logs.
- Use independent strategies for spelling, for example, analogy (if they can spell *plight* they should be able to spell *might*).
- Develop their knowledge of word patterns derived from different parts of speech as an aid to spelling, for example, *medical, medicine, medicinal, medicated.*
- Use a word bank and dictionary effectively.

- Investigate how words change when *er*, *est* and *y* are added.
- Use shortened forms correctly, for example *can't*, *won't*.
- Spell common homophones, for example, *their* and *there*, or *to*, *two* and *too*.
- Link spelling to work on grammar, for example, through an understanding of verb tenses.
- Further develop their knowledge of prefixes and suffixes.
- Spell more tricky words from Appendix 2 of the NLS.
- Investigate words with common roots as an aid to spelling, for example, *invent*, *advent*, *circumvent*.

Let's consider some of the objectives listed above that will be the focus of spelling throughout Years 3 and 4.

Identifying spelling mistakes from their writing

To do this, children need to focus on the task of checking their work. Identify which sets of words they should be checking, for example, the tricky words you wish them to notice and correct, or any words with a specific cluster or digraph that have been the focus of that week's teaching. The clearer the task is made the more focused learners will be in finding their own errors.

When teaching children to check for spelling errors, concentrate on the words that they know and can reasonably be expected to spell correctly. For example, if children have correctly spelt all the tricky words from the NLS list, these should be correct within a piece of writing. Similarly, if children have focused on a particular suffix that week (e.g. 'sion') they should be expected to reproduce that particular suffix correctly (e.g. not as 'shun') even if the rest of the word is not correct.

How are learners to know if a word is wrong? If you are sure that they have retained a particular word in their memory, simply draw attention to it and encourage them to correct the error themselves. Alternatively, some children may need to check in a wordbook or dictionary to find the correct version before they put their error right. It may sometimes appear quicker for adults to point out errors and correct them but this rather defeats the object – the point of this objective is to develop independent spellers who can put right their *own* mistakes.

Using independent spelling strategies

This objective is linked with using independent strategies for spelling. Children can only select the right spelling strategy if they have a range from which to choose. But what is a spelling strategy? It should be considered as a method for learning how to spell specific words or for working out the spelling of a new word. Some strategies may not work for all children because everybody learns differently and pupils will develop various ways of assigning spellings to their memory systems. We need to observe learners closely to decide which strategies work best for particular children.

Consider the following from which children might choose:

- Analogy – using words they know to spell new words. This may rely on children being able to identify the onsets and rimes, for example, they know how to spell *may*, so *hay, stay, play, clay* follow the same spelling pattern.
- Recognising shorter words inside longer words, for example, *the* inside *then, them, there.*
- Recalling the tricky words as part of a learned and remembered phrase with the emphasis on meaning – *he said, they can go, you are, they were.*
- Using a mnemonic, for example, *big elephants can always use small exits* (because) or *Sally Ann is dancing* (said).
- Recognising the sounds of the word in the correct sequence (e.g. *sh-o-p* as different to *p-o-sh*).
- Recognising the number of syllables in longer words and applying the knowledge that each syllable has to contain at least one vowel.
- Separating the main part of a multi-syllabic word from its prefix or suffix in order to spell the word (e.g. *measur*-ing).
- Recognising a pattern and applying a known rule.

To a large extent, children can only become independent spellers if they acquire the range of strategies that work best *for them*. Let's reflect on these strategies as we consider more of the objectives listed above.

Developing knowledge of word patterns

The purpose of this objective is to focus attention on the notion of word patterns and not solely on learning new spelling patterns. By this stage, learners have been introduced to a wide range of word patterns. Remember that spelling work in Key Stage 1 should already have covered the patterns listed below, only some of which have been explored in this book:

- All the simple words – CVC, CVCC and CCVC.
- Words with vowel digraphs.
- Other groups, for example, split vowel digraphs (the *a* and *e* are split between a consonant as in *gate, home, lime*), or vowels followed by the letter *r* (*car, part, pork, skirt, curl*).
- Words with simple endings such as *ed* and *ing*.
- Some prefixes and suffixes.

While many children will not have secured their learning of the above categories of spellings, sensitive development of word patterning will serve as reinforcement.

Let's consider word patterning at the multi-syllabic level. The strategy of separating the main part of a word from its prefix and suffix is a crucial one. Learning to spell multi-syllabic words correctly involves a highly sophisticated level of thinking about **language patterns** as well as **spelling patterns**. Complete understanding of how words are used in spoken language is vital to success at this level.

Consider the following sets of words:

inform, informing, informed, informative, information
reduce, reduced, reducing, reduction
expand, expanded, expanding, expansion
develop, developing, developed, development, developmental
invest, investigate, investigation, investigative, investigated, investigating

Which words are nouns? Which words have been formed into adjectives? Which ones are verbs, and of these, which would form part of a present tense verb structure and which would form part of a past tense verb structure? What is different about the last spelling pattern from a language perspective?

If we (or children) were doing an investigation, we might conclude that the nouns from the above list all have *sion* or *tion* or *ment* as a suffix and, therefore, words with these suffixes are highly likely to be nouns. Investigative work is an important element of learning about word patterns.

What is different about the last spelling pattern? Again, an investigative group debate might question the meaning of *invest* and identify it as the odd one out from the rest of that set as the basic meaning is different from that of *investigate*. Children need to be asking these kinds of questions if they are to develop and link their knowledge about language and spelling patterns at this complex level. They can only do this by collecting many different words, preferably from across the curriculum, as these are more likely to be words they understand as part of their subject-based learning.

Syllable awareness is also crucial to success. First, learners need to identify how many syllables the word contains before they can link this with their knowledge of prefixes and suffixes. To develop their knowledge of word patterns, children could sort words into categories. How would you categorise the words listed below?

beaker / object / information / splatter / illustrate / composition / palette / graphic / magnetic / electric / investigation / mixing

Much depends on the range of words that children collect from different subject lessons. They need to be responsible for bringing words to the session to be analysed and talked about. Talk is important here as so much of the development of spelling at this stage with the focus on word patterns relies on the meanings of words within sentences. Children whose language skills are not sufficiently developed at multi-syllabic level will have great difficulty in accessing the associated work and in achieving the above spelling objectives.

Try collecting words from the subjects you are involved with and categorise them into prefix and suffix patterns, or other forms of pattern. Analyse the words in terms of both language (meaning) and spelling. The very act of *studying words* will help you to see the complexity of what children have to deal with and enable you to design the right strategies to support them.

Using word lists and word dictionaries

Also throughout Years 3 and 4, children are taught to use a word bank or dictionary effectively. Once introduced, dictionary work needs to be re-inforced regularly. Children need to know the purpose of different dictionaries and how to find a word in order to check a spelling. Clearly, the beginning of words is crucial to this outcome. Being able to recognise CVC beginnings in words such as *habitat, memory, materials, chapter* or *computer* is essential, as is recognising consonant digraphs and clusters in longer words – *crunching, stitches* or *drafting*. Similarly, being able to identify the correct prefix within a word is essential to dictionary work.

In general, knowledge of the first three or four letters often enables us to find a desired word, but until the transitional level of spelling takes over from the phonetic level, children can also benefit from being taught to use the ACE dictionary (see Resources).

Recognising how words change when particular endings are added

What strategy supports the knowledge of how words change when letter groups are added, for example, *er, est* and *y*? We might refer to the above section on investigations. The strategy here is for learners to study a range of examples from which they can spot both a spelling and a language pattern and thus devise a rule that will apply (apart from the exceptions). How do children learn to apply a spelling rule? Consider the following words, all with *er* and *est* at the end:

tiger / mildest / warmest
anger / hardest / danger
banger / earliest / endanger
tender / tenderest / test
longer / longest / latest

I have merely listed words in these groups as they tumbled from my mind in order to form a list similar to one that children might come up with for analysis. First, if you simply ask children to find words with *er* and *est* at the end they will suggest some that are not part of this level of learning, for example, *test* is not a word with *est* as its **morphemic** ending (*test* can stand alone as a word). So we need to dump words in this category as from a language perspective they are odd ones out. They may also suggest words that are not real words at all. My computer placed a red line under 'tenderest' indicating that it isn't a word (should be 'most tender'), but I've deliberately left it in as an example of what we might expect from pupils.

Which are nouns and which are adjectives? *Tiger, anger, banger* and *danger* are nouns, all ending in *er*, but *er* is not an ending that is placed at the end of the root word. Again, these types of words do not fit as the part of the word without *er* cannot stand alone (*tig…, ang…, bang…, dang …*) within the same category of meaning. So we need to discard these too (from the discussion of *er* as a morphemic ending). We then have *longer, longest, mildest, latest* and so on, which belong to the category of **comparative adjectives**.

> long / longer / longest
> hard / harder / hardest
> late / later / latest

From each of these sets we can now see a clear pattern emerge. But which set is different from the rest? You have probably already spotted that *late, later* and *latest* involve a change in the spelling of *late* as the endings are added. You may wish to complete this analysis by determining if there are any other categories in which the root word changes when either of these endings is added at the end (I say 'end' because of words such as *est*ablished).

From this brief analysis you can see that language and meaning are the key factors that enable children to think about the spellings for these types of words. You can also see the pitfalls.

Spelling shortened forms of words

Some examples of shortened forms are shown in the box below. Children need to know from which two words these have been shortened. For example, that *can't* is a short form of *cannot*. We might draw attention to the letters that are missing in the shortened version. Meaning is crucial to children's understanding of how to use these particular versions in their sentences when writing independently.

Examples of shortened forms		
are not / aren't	cannot / can't	could not / couldn't
he is / he's	he will / he'll	he would / he'd
I am / I'm	I have / I've	I would / I'd
it is / it's	it will / it'll	let us / let's
she had / she'd	that is / that's	they are / they're
was not / wasn't	we are / we're	we had / we'd
where is / where's	will not / won't	you are / you're
you have / you've	you will / you'll	you would / you'd

We also need to point out that not all shortened forms merely lose the *n* and/or the *o*. What about the shortening of *will not* to *won't*?

Spelling common homophones

How can we help children to spell common **homophones**? We are all familiar with children's confusions between *their* and *there*, *two*, *too* and *to*, as well as *hear* and *here*. There is no magic wand – all we can do is to stress the meaning of each word within sentences and to teach the spellings of these explicitly using visual strategies (remember the LSCWC method explained earlier). Some examples of homophones are listed below. Children could be encouraged to remember these words as part of a phrase or sentence as this will help to fix the meaning to support the spelling.

Examples of homophones			
too / two / to	their / there	hear / here	broach / brooch
hair / hare	leek / leak	bare / bear	been / bean
way / whey	red / read	male / mail	be / bee
see / sea	sale / sail		

(NB: The list reminds us why children must develop visual approaches to spelling.)

So far in this chapter, we have seen clearly that spelling development throughout Years 3 and 4 must be linked to work on grammar and sentence level work. How do we know if 'there' is the right version in a particular sentence? The focus, in relation to spelling, on multi-syllabic words is all part of a necessary shift from phonic to visual approaches, which in turn supports each learner's progression from the phonetic to the transitional phase of spelling.

Spelling throughout Years 5 and 6

The final main section of this chapter considers some of the NLS objectives for developing spelling in Years 5 to 6. We need to think about these in relation to what has been said so far. Children are expected to:

- Examine words ending in vowels other than *e*, for example, *plasma, hero*.

- Investigate and classify spelling patterns in pluralisation – *s* and *es* (*buses*), *y* to *ies* (*fairy* to *fairies*) and *f* to *ves* (*hoof* to *hooves*).

- Investigate spellings and meanings of more prefixes (e.g. *auto, bi, trans*) and suffixes (e.g. *cian* in *electrician*).

- Spell possessive pronouns, for example, *theirs* and *yours*.

- Spell words with unstressed vowels, for example, *poisonous, freedom, extra*.

- Explore word roots with their prefixes and suffixes, for example, *aero*plane, *micro*scope.

The objectives throughout Year 6 make increasing references to *spelling through other English work* with the need to link spelling work with grammar. The point has been made, but needs to be emphasised, that the basics of learning to spell need to be accomplished in Key Stage 1 as far as possible. Those children who have not acquired the foundations before they move to Key Stage 2 will find it extremely difficult to access a highly demanding programme of spelling and grammar work linked to the rules and conventions of English writing. In this context, the companion book in this series *Supporting Writing* has a wealth of advice on supporting writing development.

This and the previous two chapters have emphasised the crucial importance of children mastering letter patterns as the basis of spelling development. Being able to hear sounds, identify these as phonemes within words and to match them to the correct choice of graphemes alongside a developing perception of language gradually emerges as a colourful patch-work of understanding. It must be remembered that however finely tuned our phonological awareness becomes, and this must never be neglected, in order to become 'good' spellers we must recognise when it is the right time for visual strategies to become dominant. As children move into that transitional phase, we need to strengthen the visual skills that will guide them towards independence in spelling. Learners whose visual strategies do not eventually dominate their thinking will never reach that final stage of coping with the many irregularities of English spelling, for example:

- Do I need *there* or *their* in this sentence?
- How do I spell *said, who* or *because?*
- What about *rough, bough* and *although? Ruff, bow* and *allthow* could be likely choices if phonetic spelling continues to dominate.

The answers to the spelling dilemmas above are strictly visual and language-based.

As mentioned in Chapter 3, memory is also crucial to success. Time spent on memory training is well worth the effort and will pay dividends. Much of the spelling work done in classrooms will be an ongoing part of the weekly routine and is highly likely to reflect some differentiation of the teaching objectives at age-expected levels. Alongside this mainly class-based work, additional time will always be necessary for those children who need to revisit objectives from earlier years to secure them.

In Year 6, we could find that:

- A small proportion of learners are still not confident with segmenting sounds to spell CVC words.
- A larger group may not have secured the spelling of CCVC or CVCC words.
- A significantly larger group have not mastered the spelling of all vowel digraphs.
- A further large group do not fully understand the work on prefixes and suffixes.

- In addition, many children will not be able to spell all the high-frequency words from the NLS lists (from Reception level through to Years 3 and 4).

So what can schools do? All we can do is track back to earlier NLS objectives and attempt to fill in significant gaps in skills and knowledge as they are identified for individual pupils.

Summary

In this chapter I have looked at:

- The NLS objectives for spelling for Years 3 to 6.
- Support strategies for developing the key skills required to meet the objectives.

Chapter 7

Assessing and monitoring spelling progress

Previous chapters have explored the development of spelling and provided some strategies for supporting learners throughout their spelling journey. While the emphasis so far has been on how adults, particularly teaching assistants, can support the teaching and learning of spelling, we need to see how assessing spelling fits into the *plan-prepare-deliver-review* cycle and the role of the teaching assistant.

Consider the curriculum cycle in relation to spelling:

- *Planning* – deciding on the objectives, differentiating the content for various groups and individuals. Deciding what strategies and resources are to be used.

- *Preparation* – assembling and/or preparing the materials and resources needed to deliver the planned work for whole classes/groups or individuals.

- *Delivery* – what actually happens in the classroom, i.e. teaching, supporting, learning.

- *Review* – assessing the learning and asking the question: to what extent have all children learned what was *planned* for them to learn?

Ideally, the review should then inform the next planning stage after having considered how well children have learned what has been taught. The focus of this chapter is to link the review element of the cycle to the idea of assessing pupils and monitoring their progress.

Many teaching assistants play a significant role in assessment and monitoring. Bearing in mind what we have so far covered in this book about spelling, consider the following questions:

- How do we assess the spelling competence of individual learners and monitor their progress over time?
- How can learners be helped to assess their own spelling progress?
- Against what criteria might we assess our support of spelling?

The rest of this chapter addresses these questions.

What is assessment?

The word 'assessment' has many interpretations. A recent government document *Removing Barriers to Achievement* (DfES 2004) emphasises the key role of assessment for learning. What does this mean in terms of our support? If we assume that assessment is a key part of the teaching and learning cycle (the review), then the prime purpose is to inform curriculum planning, which in turn should maximise the learning experience for all children.

Standardised tests

Consider the traditional approaches to assessing spelling, often in the form of **standardised tests**. Such tests offer a spelling age that is of little use to inform planning, therefore they do not support learning. What do you understand by a spelling age of 7.6 or 9.3? Some of us may be able to link this with a rough level of spelling, but such a score tells us little about the strengths and weaknesses of individual learners. Similarly, knowing that a pupil has a spelling **quotient** of 84 does not help adults to set up a learning programme – such information merely informs us that a child is below average. Standardised tests have their uses, but are not part of 'assessment for learning'.

Purposes for assessment

In general, assessment can be used to:

- Assess and monitor individual pupil achievement.
- Evaluate achievement at whole-school level.

- Monitor and compare the achievements of different schools and compile national data to inform government decision-making (e.g. SATs).

With regard to the role of the teaching assistant, the rest of this chapter will now focus on:

- Assessment for learning.
- Using assessment to monitor pupil progress.
- Using assessment to set up an intervention programme.
- Pupils' self-assessment.
- Record-keeping.

Assessment for learning

In the context of spelling, how far do you agree that assessment should:

- Identify what children can do as well as what they can't?
- Include a range of evidence from across the curriculum?
- Cater for the diversity of learning styles?
- Include a range of views of what children can do – from school staff, external agencies where relevant, parents and the pupils themselves?
- Measure the progress of each child against him or herself, not against others?
- Be manageable?

Most of you will hopefully agree with the above points in principle, but practice often deviates from them. For example, how often does assessment (of spelling?) measure what children cannot do, perhaps creating feelings of failure, rather than what they can do, thus promoting perceptions of success? Similarly, how often are our assessments of spelling based on limited evidence, for example, a Monday morning spelling test? How far do we involve others in assessing spelling competence, for example, parents or the children themselves?

Who should be involved?

If assessment is to support learning, then it should include all those who are involved in a child's learning programme – teachers, teaching assistants, external specialists, parents and, crucially important, the learners themselves.

What can staff assess and how?

- *Standardised testing* – there is nothing wrong in using standardised tests providing we recognise the limitations of the results, but if a below-average score is identified, schools must then diagnose the learner's difficulties and set up a catch-up programme to address them.
- *Informal spelling tests* – for example, the high-frequency words from the NLS lists. Such tests are often referred to as **criterion-referenced**. We might allocate 20 minutes each week for testing the spelling work that has been taught. These types of assessment inform us if children have retained what has been taught, but done in isolation they cannot tell us if children are using what they know in other spelling contexts.
- *Spelling within the context of writing* – those of us who have observed children applying their spelling knowledge in other subjects will know that many fail to transfer learning across the curriculum. A child may spell 'said' correctly on the spelling test, but then produce 'sed' when writing a story. In my view, the child has not learned to spell 'said' as he/she is not doing so in a *real* spelling situation. Observing spelling across the curriculum is the most useful and informative type of assessment that we can all be part of, as long as we record and use the data to support the review and inform the planning part of the next cycle.

What can parents assess and how?

Admittedly parents are limited in what they can assess in spelling; however, the involvement of parents in the spelling process is vital to a child's success. Parents could be informed of the level their child has reached in spelling so that they can reinforce this through homework. If parents know that their child can spell the first 45 words on the high-frequency NLS lists (and are given a copy), they are more likely to point out mistakes when supervising homework sessions. Similarly, if parents know that their child can use a dictionary to check the spelling of difficult words, they are in a better position to reinforce this skill rather than simply giving spellings on request.

In accordance with the school's parental involvement policy, many teaching assistants liaise with parents on a regular basis and are in a position to inform parents of the level of spelling their child has reached. Occasionally, as part of that informal liaison or at IEP reviews, parents could be given examples of words on which their child needs to focus, for example, a list of the high-frequency words or the vowel digraphs. All too often, informal conversations with parents don't get to the heart of how they could help their child's learning.

Assuming that we have informed parents about their child's progress in spelling, a few tips are always helpful. For example, parents could be reminded to:

● Always write down words then cover them for the child to spell from memory (show parents how to support the LSCWC method).

● Draw attention to little words within longer ones.

● Draw attention to letter strings – on TV adverts, on car number plates and so on.

● Identify the part of a word that is right before making any corrections.

● Enjoy the content of writing and praise this before talking about the spelling.

● Not correct every mistake, but focus on those that are linked to their child's current phase of learning.

Assessing the learning environment

An inclusive approach to spelling would ensure that all children:

● Have access to the spelling curriculum through work that is differentiated to suit their needs.

● Are presented with suitable spelling challenges at the right level – neither too easy, nor too hard.

● Are given opportunities to learn according to their optimum learning styles, for example, by being given a range of strategies from which to choose.

The National Curriculum inclusion statements invite us to ask questions about the learning environment that we have provided for spelling. Are we taking account of different learning styles (celebrating diversity)? Can all learners access and learn from the objectives for this week or do they need to backtrack to earlier ones? Periodically, we may need to assess the teaching and the support of spelling as well as pupils' learning.

Using assessment to monitor progress

What do we mean by progress and how much progress can individual pupils reasonably be expected to make? If a pupil has increased a spelling **quotient** from 85 to 94, what does this tell us? Is it enough for that pupil? This depends on what we know about that child. If a quotient has been increased, this means that a child has caught up to some degree, even if he/she is still below the average (of 100). Some children with learning difficulties may never attain quotients within the average range, therefore an increased quotient of one or two points may represent excellent progress.

Similarly, over a year, an increase in spelling age from 7.6 to 7.9 may be reasonable for some pupils with identified learning difficulties, but for others may indicate underachievement. Consider the criteria by which we often measure spelling, for example, the NLS high-frequency words. If 10 per cent were spelled correctly at the last IEP review and 60 per cent are now spelled correctly, is this reasonable progress? For some this may be excellent, for others, not enough.

What if assessment results actually decrease? For some, the reasons may be linked to the child's emotional state – family problems such as divorce or bereavement may affect some children's learning more than we realise. However, schools must also question if the learning environment has been right for a particular child. Returning to the three statements on inclusion, have barriers to learning been removed to allow access to teaching? Has that child's diversity been recognised and the right spelling strategies put in place? Have the learning challenges been suitable for that particular child?

Only by knowing children as *learners* can we use spelling assessments to monitor rates of progress and decide if any new intervention, or changes to the same intervention, may need to be made. Assessment for learning implies that we analyse and challenge the results that we obtain.

Using assessment to set up an intervention programme

Assuming that a child has not made reasonable progress, what should we do? If the child has learning difficulties and is already receiving additional intervention as stated in the *Revised Code of Practice for Special Educational Needs* (DfES 2001) either at School Action (from within the school's resources only) or at School Action Plus (using external resources via an SEN support service), then the intervention strategies will be identified at an IEP review. Progress will be discussed and the next set of targets decided upon.

The IEP review meeting should include both parents and pupils as part of the decision-making process so that they can be informed of spelling progress and invited to contribute to the intervention strategies. As a teaching assistant how closely are you involved in IEP reviews? Teaching assistants can make a substantial contribution to IEP decision-making as they are more likely to know pupils as learners than any other member of the school staff, especially if they have worked with and coached children as individuals or in small groups.

What if progress is not being made and the child does not have identified learning difficulties? If you suspect that a child is not making progress at a rate that seems right for him/her, then talk to the class teacher – it may be that the child needs to be further assessed in order to diagnose the extent and nature of the problem. This more detailed type of assessment is often called diagnostic as it identifies the source of the difficulty and helps to pinpoint what can be done to address it. The special educational needs co-ordinator (SENCO) may need to be involved together with any external specialists as necessary. It may be decided that the child merely needs to be monitored more closely or that a School Action type of intervention is needed, for example, a daily session on some identified area of spelling.

More significantly, if the initial intervention is not seen to improve progress, then the school may decide to:

- Operate further or different School Action intervention as appropriate.
- Seek the services of an external SEN agency for advice (School Action Plus).
- Consult the local education authority (LEA) educational psychologist for more specialised assessment.

For a tiny percentage of children, the outcome may result in further specialised assessment by the LEA to see if a **statement for SEN** is necessary (for those children for whom many interventions have been tried but not resulted in any significant progress).

The input from teaching assistants is critical to the effectiveness of the assessment and monitoring process, alongside and with individual children. This brings us to the important question of how and to what extent all pupils can be involved in the assessment and monitoring of their own progress, particularly with regard to spelling.

Pupils' self-assessment

However strongly the notion of pupil participation is stressed – and we all agree with this principle – the key question is 'how'? Strategies for involving children in their own spelling development could include the following:

- First, make sure that children understand their own levels or targets, i.e. each success criteria and how success is to be measured. Objectives could be written in spelling workbooks using child-friendly language with which the children are familiar.
- Train children how to recognise when a high-frequency word is wrong – ask the child if it 'looks right'. If children are using their visual strategies to spell these words, they should be acquiring a sixth sense and noticing if it looks wrong.
- Try not to always correct spellings yourself – you could underline the whole word or part of a word for children then ask them to study it and see if they can improve on it. Offer clues but try to encourage children to spot the error themselves.
- My own words – analyse together the words a child spells wrongly having picked out the words to be focused and try to determine what

the error signifies. For example, does it suggest confusion of particular consonant clusters or one of the vowel digraph families? Does it indicate a significant problem with phonological awareness?

- Talk about the difficulties with the child and decide how you are *both* going to tackle them. Hopefully the errors will have included spelling from different subject areas and should be addressed as such. For example, after some discussion and reinforcement of key knowledge, you may both agree that the child will spell all words starting with *sh* or *ch* with *those particular graphemes* correctly.

- Try to place some responsibility for solving the problem with the child according to age and any identified learning difficulty.

- Try to move beyond the generalities of simply saying that their spelling is 'good' or 'better'. With practice, most children can be encouraged to talk about the details of their spelling. How is it better? What are they doing now that they were not doing last week/term/year? In this way they can take far more responsibility for achieving their own objectives.

Some dos and don'ts when working with children to assess spellings

- Remember the principle of spellings being 'somewhere along the road to rightness'.

- Be sensitive – try not to point out every spelling mistake as this can demotivate children. Focus only on those that are significant.

- Never give children a word to copy – write it down or let them find it in a dictionary, then ask them to write from memory (LSCWC strategy).

- Remind children who are struggling that learning to spell is a long process and they are not expected to get everything right at once. Always find something to praise before talking about improvements required.

Involving children in monitoring their own progress

Strategies could include:

- Comparing last term/year's writing with what they are doing now. Talk about why the spellings are improved.

- Make it visual and let them see the improvements by keeping a (dated) portfolio of writing.
- Highlight particular examples to illustrate points in a bright colour to encourage children to focus on the areas of progress.
- Be positive – always point out the progress before going on to identify areas where improvements are still needed. If offered sensitively, children can learn to accept criticism without losing their self-esteem.

Keeping records and analysing data

What types of spelling records do you maintain? Do you complete a photocopied sheet or do you record data in a diary? However you record the information, keep it brief and to the point. Only note down significant information that is related to:

- The child's stage of spelling, e.g. emergent or semi-phonetic.
- Spelling targets on which you and the child are working.
- The skills and knowledge the child has acquired.
- The strategies the child uses to spell.
- Whether (from cross-curricular observations) the child is applying his/her spelling knowledge as part of writing.

Below are some examples of what might be recorded.

Joshua (Year 1): part of the report for his IEP review

Joshua's spelling is improving. He can spell approximately 20 per cent of words from the NLS high-frequency list for the Reception year. He writes most of the individual letters and recognises the sounds, but cannot yet match the names to each letter. When writing, he often identifies and writes the first letter in a new word. Joshua struggles to segment phonemes to spell CVC words and has not secured the digraphs *sh*, *ch* and *th*.

Joshua is falling behind in all areas and needs intervention strategies. At what developmental spelling phase would you place Joshua? What might his next set of targets be for spelling?

Lewis (Year 4): summary of teaching assistant's record notes

Lewis spells almost all high-frequency words from Reception and approx. 60 per cent of those from the Year 1 to Year 2 lists. He spells many single-syllable words up to vowel digraph level, and clearly identifies syllables in words. He has minimal knowledge of the spelling of prefixes and suffixes.

What sort of picture does this suggest for Lewis's progress? What phase of spelling development has he reached and what might be his next targets?

Jasmine (Year 5): notes from teaching assistant's records

Jasmine can spell most of the high-frequency words from the NLS lists. She confuses *sh* and *ch* and represents the sound *th* as *f*. Her phonological awareness is weak and she often represents sounds randomly rather than strategically when trying new words.

What does Jasmine need in order to move her spelling on?

Continual, cumulative or summative?

Record-keeping is a highly important area. What happens to the records you have made? How can we handle the volume over time? On a continual level, records need to be kept of where children are, what programme they are on and what skills and knowledge they have acquired (or not acquired) on a daily or at least a weekly basis. These are the types of records that fuel ongoing discussions among key staff involved with children's spelling programmes.

Who are these records for? Perhaps you feel that these records are mainly for yourself and whoever is sharing responsibility for spelling development with you. These ongoing records guide the work you are doing and the associated liaison. Cumulatively, such records can build up into a huge file, the contents of which need to be summarised for IEP or annual review meetings with parents. Once the key information has been extracted from continual and bulky data, it then becomes more manageable. The bulk of continual data could then be dispensed with once it has been summarised into a cumulative form. This cumulative record-keeping can become part of the child's personal, developmental records to be seen by anyone who needs to be involved (remembering data protection), parents or even by the child. In this sense they are more formal than the rough notes we make on a continual basis.

There are times when we may need to summarise records for particular purposes, for example, on transition between schools, key stages or to form part of annual reports to parents. You may make a contribution at this level too. When preparing records, at whatever level:

- Stick to the facts, not opinions.
- Be sensitive – remember that parents and learners may have access to what you write.
- Be clear and systematic and always date records of any kind.
- Keep information focused and relevant to the child's objectives and responses.

Finally in this section, we might usefully ask what needs to be done for Joshua, Lewis and Jasmine whose records (for spelling only) are featured above. How would we help these children, and what could the intervention strategies include for each one?

Analysing the records

So, what do we need to do for each of these learners? In which direction does their spelling need to be guided?

Joshua

It would appear that Joshua is roughly at semi-phonetic level. His spelling targets might be selected from the following:

- To spell 50 per cent of the high-frequency words on the Reception year list.
- To identify initial and final phonemes in three-letter CVC words and segment these to spell.
- To spell four-letter CVC words.
- To secure the digraphs *sh* and *ch*.

The strategy to enable Joshua to achieve his targets could include:

- The teaching assistant working on these for a few minutes each day.
- The parents working on the high-frequency words (having been given a copy).
- 'Buddy' work – Joshua could take responsibility for choosing and learning 5 (or 10 or 15) high-frequency words each week and asking his assigned buddy to check these with him each Friday afternoon.

Joshua could learn and check the high-frequency words himself, but let's assume that he is more of a 'social' learner and needs peer support to motivate him.

Lewis

We might assume that Lewis is verging on transitional level and represents a range of graphemes in his spelling. His targets could be selected from:

- Consolidation of vowel digraph word patterns.
- Learning particular spellings for prefixes and suffixes.
- Learning to spell all the words from the NLS high-frequency lists.

The strategy for Lewis could be similar to that for Joshua. Both he and his parents need to be included. The intervention model needs to link with class-based work on prefixes and suffixes and should be language-focused.

Jasmine

Jasmine appears to be spelling at semi-phonetic level (random rather than strategic). Her profile is unusual in that she can spell many of the tricky words, suggesting that her visual skills are stronger but her phonic skills and phonological awareness need to be addressed. Her targets might be selected from:

- Securing the phonemes/graphemes *sh* and *ch*.
- Learning to spell words with *th*.
- Sequencing sounds in words and representing these strategically in spelling.

Strategies might include:

- The teaching assistant to work on sound sequences in words and *sh*, *ch* and *th*.
- Jasmine to find above examples from across the curriculum and bring to the intervention sessions.
- Parents to support Jasmine's phonic objectives.

Let the spellings speak!

Finally in this chapter, remember that assessment for learning is all about being able to analyse spelling errors and to help children to learn from them. Let's look briefly at some misspellings in general. Sometimes we need to let the words speak as they often inform us how children are thinking about spelling.

What do the following spellings tell us about the learners? Which spellers are almost there? Which spellers have a long way to go?

mist (missed)	busis (buses)	sed (said)	shud (should)
happing (happening)	wif (with)	brecfust (breakfast)	murls (marbles)
woz (was)	tabul (table)	clime (climb)	krakuz (crackers)
choklut (chocolate)	spas (space)	sayl (sale)	copoot (computer)
randyeer (reindeer)	bot (bought)	wiy (why)	roodolf (Rudolph)
ascrim (ice cream)	vidoy (video)	leeph (leaf)	pratsing (practising)

The child who spells 'leeph' for leaf and 'clime' for climb has retained a range of graphemes and is representing these in his/her spelling. What do you think about this example: Berysentedmends? Can you work it out? (Clue – it's a town in England.) You've no doubt got it – Bury St Edmunds. Clearly, this learner has developed excellent phonological awareness and this needs to be matched by a range of phonic knowledge. I'll leave you to think about the rest of these examples and to form your conclusions.

Summary

In this chapter I have looked at:

- The *plan-prepare-deliver-review* cycle of teaching for learning.
- Record-keeping.
- Assessment and monitoring of spelling.
- How we can use cross-curricular data to support a rounded judgement of progress.
- The involvement of learners themselves.
- The substantial contribution teaching assistants can make to the effectiveness of the school's assessment and monitoring system.

Conclusion

This book has explored the skills and knowledge associated with spelling, and outlined how most learners can progress towards becoming competent and independent spellers. We have noted how the teaching and learning of spelling is led by the objectives listed in the NLS framework.

It is important to remember that not all learners do become competent spellers. For a range of reasons, many people still cannot spell well into adulthood. The key principles for developing competent spellers identified in Chapter 3 underpin the specific work on the spelling objectives explored in Chapters 4 to 6. In my view, applying these principles could, for some children, mean the difference between success and failure.

Spelling is such a complex area of development for a great many young people that without these principles, supported by a sensitive and positive learning environment, learning to spell can seem like a distant dream, or at worst, a nightmare. Our dream is surely to enable success for as many children as possible, so that they can feel good about themselves as developing spellers.

Whether you are an inexperienced teaching assistant or aspiring to become one of the growing numbers of higher-level teaching assistants, I hope that this book has met your needs and that it has offered much food for thought about spelling, at whatever level you are working. Perhaps the information contained and the strategies suggested have provided you with some further dimensions to support your thinking about spelling and about helping children to become independent spellers.

References

DfEE (1995) *English in the National Curriculum.* London: HMSO.

DfES (2001) *Revised Code of Practice for Special Educational Needs.* London: DfES.

DfES (2003) *Excellence and Enjoyment.* London: DfES.

DfES (2004) *Removing Barriers to Achievement.* London: DfES.

Edwards, S. (2004) *Supporting Writing.* London: David Fulton Publishers.

Gentry, J.R. (1987) *Spel- Is a Four-Letter Word.* Leamington Spa: Scholastic.

Given, B.K. and Reid, G. (1999) *Learning Styles: A Guide for Teachers and Parents.* St. Annes on Sea: Red Rose Publications.

National Literacy Strategy (2001) *National Literacy Strategy Framework for Teaching.* London: DfES.

Resources

Identifying resources for supporting spelling is a daunting task – nothing can take the place of a skilled and sensitive adult as a human resource! The following list includes materials that cover many areas of spelling referred to in this book. Some are intended as reinforcement to allow children to practise what has already been taught.

For letter learning

- A set of wooden, plastic, raised or 'furry' letters (to feel) in lower case.
- The same in upper case.
- A set which shows *ch*, *sh* and *th* as single phonemes.
- A set which shows the consonant clusters or the vowel digraphs (*cl, dr, ea, oi*) joined together to emphasise the BME principle.
- A set that shows the vowels and consonants in different colours – the LDA 'word building box' contains black consonants and red vowels and has enough letters for building a few short sentences.

Workbooks and useful resources for adults

Photocopiable worksheets or workbooks can be useful for homework tasks or for practising the skills that have been taught. They are not intended for use as a main spelling resource – that role is reserved for the human resources! Try the following:

- *Don't Forget the Alphabet* and *Hunt the Word* (Easylearn).

- *A Hand for Spelling* is an old favourite that combines spelling and hand-writing and will take pupils through to the transitional stage of spelling (LDA).
- *Searchlights for Spelling* – covers NLS objectives and is cross-referenced to the *Phonic Progression* booklet (Cambridge University Press).
- *Phonic Progression* (DfES) contains games at every spelling level – a must for adults who are involved with spelling development.
- The Key Stage 2 spelling bank contains banks of useful words for every level, with suggestions for how to develop some of the spelling objectives (DfES 1999).

Interactive materials

The following resources are worth checking out as they are mainly interactive, multisensory and will help to keep children motivated. Some are also self-checking and can help to develop children's independence in general.

For Key Stage 1 work:

- Nursery rhymes – practice sounds and rhythms (Smart Kids).
- Initial letter sounds – 'objects' bag (LDA).
- Brickworks word-building games (LDA).
- Sound beginnings – comprehensive set on letter sounds (LDA).
- Paper chains, Set 1 and Set 2 – develop word level work from CVC onwards (LDA).
- Consonant cluster dominoes game (LDA).
- Very basic bingo – to reinforce the first list of high-frequency words (Smart Kids).
- Chunks – plastic tiles for onset and rime, reinforces up to vowel digraph level (Smart Kids).
- 'Shake and make' words – onset and rime dice game and puzzle matching (LDA).
- Alliterations flip book (Smart Kids).

- High-frequency word flashcards that show the word against its 'shape' background – useful for developing visual skills (Smart Kids).
- *Let's Spell* – flip-over books that reinforce the BME principle for CVC, CCVC and CVCC words (Smart Kids).
- 'Find Your Fish' series covers all aspects of phonics – game played on a baseboard. High interest level, but needs time (Philip & Tacey).
- Phonix cubes come in a jar with the range of letters and clusters separated by colour. These are fun to use and include plastic trays for word building. A very useful general phonic resource (Philip & Tacey).
- Washing line and pegs for early letter and word work (Philip & Tacey).
- Phonix 'swap it' focuses on changing letters to make new words (Philip & Tacey).
- 'Jolly Phonics' is a comprehensive scheme for letter learning and early phonic work – fun-based and highly interactive (Jolly Learning Ltd).
- The 'Early Literacy Support' kit includes a hand puppet, letters, alphabet tapes, letter fans, flashcards, games for much multisensory work on phonics (LDA).

For Key Stage 2 work:

- THRASS – comprises a comprehensive system for developing spelling.
- Contractions – interlocking tiles and bingo game (Smart Kids).
- Cryptic compounds – 20 self-correcting word cards (Smart Kids).
- Homophones and homographs – contains examples of these words in sentences (Smart Kids).
- Prefixes and suffixes – plastic tiles on a magnetic board (Smart Kids).
- Syllabification – tiles on a magnetic board (Smart Kids).
- 'Chute' activities – place a card in the chute and see the 'answers' appear at the bottom. Pack of 50 cards – for syllables and abbreviations (Smart Kids).
- The 'Active Literacy Kit' – designed for children who have fallen behind in their literacy work as a 'way in' (LDA).

- Phonix cubes (see above) – can be continued into Key Stage 2 (Philip & Tacey).
- Phonics 'sorter' boxes – practise identifying vowel digraph patterns as children categorise the cards onto a base board (Philip & Tacey).
- Jungle series – practises compound words and prefixes (Philip & Tacey).

In addition, STILE (from LDA) comprises a set of comprehensive materials that include all the main spelling levels and are interesting for children to work on as individuals and groups. The activities are based on a self-correcting tray into which children place each tile in response to a work card. If the tiles have been placed in the tray correctly, the pattern on the reverse will be correct. The set has been around for some time, but has recently been revamped in line with the NLS objectives.

Dictionaries

These could include:

- A selection of dictionaries starting at a simple picture level.
- The ACE dictionary – particularly useful for supporting children as they move from phonetic to transitional spelling as it is structured around how words sound (LDA).

For handwriting

- Roll and write alphabet – the ball traces the correct letter formation and even retraces its path for difficult letters such as *b* and *d* (LDA).
- Grippies (for children with handwriting difficulties) – ensures that fingers are accurately placed on the pencils (LDA).
- Tri-go-grip – reduces muscle strain and ensures a comfortable hold (LDA).
- Speed-up – a kinaesthetic handwriting programme to develop fluent handwriting for children whose writing lacks fluency and speed (LDA).
- *Write from the Start* – a perceptuo-motor approach to handwriting (LDA).

▧ ICT for spelling

Resources that cover a range of spelling levels include:

- *WordShark* – a program with 36 highly motivating games to support spelling at various levels. This program is not new, but is one of those simple ICT resources that does not allow the ICT to detract from the focus on the spelling (White Space Ltd).
- *Starspell* – a simple program that does not overshadow the focus on the spelling (Fisher-Marriott).
- *My Spelling Friend* is designed to reinforce spelling in groups or individually. The games reinforce the LSCWC strategy and practise most of the letter clusters (Sherston Software).

There are numerous examples of resources that could have been added to the above list, all of which are designed to do something different. The aim is to have a range of materials to hand that will do the right job when needed. The above resources are not intended to represent a comprehensive list – they are merely some of the resources that I have found useful. When choosing resources for spelling, we need to ensure that:

- Materials for spelling do not take the place of an adult.
- The resource does what it is supposed to do (e.g. practises the objective on which it is meant to focus).
- The resources comprise a range of materials that will cater for different styles of learning – worksheets (use sparingly), interactive tiles, games and ICT where appropriate.

If you have gained the impression that I dislike the use of worksheets for developing spelling, then you are right. In my view, worksheets do little to enhance children's skills. The above list is intended to promote the use of resources for spelling that are interactive, multisensory and fun. It is also important to ensure that games do not overshadow the skills on which they may be focusing. Many games take so long to set up and are so complex that the focus on the spelling skill becomes lost within the playing of the game.

Useful addresses

Cambridge University Press, The Edinburgh Building, Shaftesbury Road, Cambridge CB2 1RU. Tel: 01223 312393; Fax: 01223 315052; http://uk.cambridge.org.

Easylearn Ltd, Trent House, Fiskerton, Southwell, Notts NG25 0UH. Tel: 01636 830240; Fax: 01636 830162; www.easylearn.co.uk.

Fisher-Marriott Software, 58 Victoria Road, Woodbridge IP12 1EL. Tel: 01394 387050; Fax: 01394 380064; www.fishmarriott.com.

Jolly Learning Ltd, Tailours House, High Road, Chigwell, Essex IG7 6DL. Tel: 020 8501 0405; Fax: 020 8500 1696; www.jollylearning.co.uk.

LDA, Duke Street, Wisbech, Cambs PE13 2AE. Tel: 01945 463441; www.LDAlearning.com.

Philip & Tacey Ltd, North Way, Andover, Hants SP10 5BA. Tel: 01264 332171; Fax: 01264 384808; www.philipandtacey.co.uk.

Sherston Software, Angel House, Sherston, Near Malmesbury, Wiltshire SN16 0LH. Tel: 01666 843200; Fax: 01666 843216; www2.sherston.com.

Smart Kids (UK) Ltd, 5 Station Road, Hungerford, Berkshire RG17 0DY. Tel: 01488 644644; Fax: 01488 644745; www.smartkids.co.uk.

THRASS (UK) Ltd, Units 1–3 Tarvin Sands, Barrow Lane, Tarvin, Chester CH3 8JF. Tel: 01829 741413; Fax: 01829 741419; www.thrass.co.uk.

White Space Ltd, 41 Mall Road, London W6 9DG. Tel/fax: 020 8748 5927.

Spelling quiz

The two wrong spellings are weild (wield) and aquiesce (acquiesce).

Glossary

Alliteration
Words with the same initial letter sound – laugh, link, like, letter.

Alphabetical order
Sequence of the 26 letters of the alphabet from a to z.

Analogies
Applying the concept of rhyme and rime to what we know about spelling, e.g. we can spell *peach* so we should be able to spell *beach, teach, reach.*

Ascenders
The 'stick' on the following letters – *b, d, f, h, k, l, t.*

Auditory discrimination
Ability to perceive differences between the sounds we hear.

Chunking
Identifying groups of letters together as a single unit or smaller words inside longer words – en*chant*ment, dis*orient*ed.

Comparative adjectives
Adjectives that compare, e.g. size or length – *tall, taller, tallest, wide, wider, widest.*

Consonant
All letters except *a, e, i, o, u* are consonants.

Criterion-referenced tests
Assess against identified criteria, e.g. high-frequency words or particular phonic knowledge. They are not standardised.

CVC words
Three- or four-letter words, each with three phonemes and a short medial vowel – *cat, ship, push, chip, mat.*

Descenders
The 'tails' that fall below the line when the following letters are written – *g, j, p, q, y.*

External specialist
Person from outside the school (LEA or health department) whose specialist knowledge (e.g. in autism, dyslexia, speech and language) as additional

	SEN provision may be sought in order to address learning difficulties.
Grammar	Structural rules of a language that govern writing in Standard English and inform spelling.
Grapheme	Letters and letter clusters that represent phonemes (sounds) in words, e.g. *ea, ie* and *ee* can all represent one phoneme.
Grapheme combinations	Refer to the range of different graphemes that can match the same phoneme.
High-frequency words	Words that are the most commonly used for writing and spelling – listed in the NLS framework for teaching. Many of these words need to be learned visually.
Homophones	Words that sound exactly the same but have a different meaning and spelling – *here/hear, be/bee, sea/see, herd/heard.*
Investigation	Strategy for finding out about things by collecting examples with the same given criterion (e.g. spelling patterns) and reaching conclusions.
Language patterns	The range of ways in which words and sentences can be combined to form language.
Learning difficulty	This term stems from the Code of Practice (DfES 2001). Children have a learning difficulty if they learn more slowly or with greater difficulty than the majority of children of the same age.
Letter strings	Combinations of letters within words that combine for spelling – *br* as in *brush, str* as in *string, sh* as in *shoot, ought* as in *thought.*
LSCWC	Look, Say, Cover, Write, Check – strategy for learning how to spell words visually. *See also* Visual approach.
Morphemic ending	Group of letters placed at the end of a word that alters its form – the *es* in *buses* or the *ing* in *holding.*
Non-word	Combination of letters that fits a phonic pattern logically without being a real word – *hab, pom, sim* are all CVC patterns but without meaning.

Onset and rime	Describes spelling patterns where the beginnings and ends of words are spelled the same – *beach, teach, reach*, or *shoot, boot, hoot*.
Perception	What the brain interprets from the senses.
Phonemes	Sounds within words that can be segmented for spelling – *sh* in ship, *oo* in pool, *ea* in peach.
Phonetic approach	Using phonological awareness and phonic knowledge to spell words on the basis of sound.
Phonic knowledge	Knowing the range of graphemes (letters and letter clusters) that can be matched to their phonemes (sounds in words).
Phonological awareness	Understanding of the general relationship between sounds in words and the letters that are used to spell them.
Phonological patterns	Refer to the sounds of letters within a word.
Prefixes	Groups of letters placed at the beginning of words that can alter the meaning, class and grammatical form to make a new word – *em*power, *re*view, *dis*member, *im*probable. Prefixes cannot stand alone as words.
Quotient	Age-related measure of attainment – average is usually 100.
Rhyming	Words with only the beginning that sounds different – *tea, bee* and *key / hear* and *beer*.
Segment	To separate sounds within words in order to spell them.
Sound out	To say the word and separate each sound within the word.
Sound–symbol relationship	Matching of letter shapes (graphemes) to letter sounds (phonemes).
Special educational need	From the Code of Practice (DfES 2001), children have SEN if they have a learning difficulty and their needs require additional provision to be made from within the school or from external resources.
Spelling patterns	The range of ways in which letters can combine to form words.

Standard English	Variety of English employed by educated users (e.g. the media).
Standardised tests	Tests that have been validated on a sample of children. These tests often give a score in the form of a quotient and/or are age-related.
Statement	Children who are assessed by an LEA as having significant learning difficulties may be allocated a statement. Statements often signify additional resources.
Suffixes	Common letter groups placed at the ends of words that can alter the meaning, class and grammatical form to make a new word – power*ed*, probabil*ity*, enchant*ment*. Suffixes cannot stand alone as words.
Syllables	Can be thought of as 'beats' within a word. Each syllable in English has one vowel sound (could be a vowel digraph) – *house* has one syllable, *table* has two, *computer* has three, *entertainment* has four. Multi-syllabic words are those with more than one syllable.
Upper case letters	Capital letters, e.g. the letters *H, A, P, Q, R.*
Visual approach	Learning to spell by studying what the whole word looks like not the sounds within the word.
Visual discrimination	Ability to perceive differences from what we see, e.g. between shapes, pictures, letters and numbers.
Vowel	The letters *a, e, i, o* and *u* are all vowels. All other letters are consonants.
Vowel digraphs	Vowels that combine into a single sound, e.g. the letters *ai, oi, ee, ea, oo* as in *rain, boil, peel, peach, shoot*. Sometimes called long vowel phonemes.
Word, sentence and text	Refers to the cumulative nature of language as we combine words into sentences, and sentences into longer pieces of writing. Texts can be thought of as any item of print, e.g. books, magazines, leaflets and newspapers.

Index